THE BADREDHEAD MEDIA
30-DAY BOOK
MARKETING CHALLENGE

RACHEL THOMPSON

CONTENTS

PART III
WEEK THREE

PART IV
WEEK FOUR

INTRODUCTION

Hello, Challenge Takers! Rachel here (aka *BadRedhead Media*). So proud of you for taking on this challenge -- you can do this! Book marketing (or blog or business) can be overwhelming. I know -- I've done all three, and still do all three every single day. I feel you.

Who is BadRedhead Media?

Here's my deal: After 17+ years in soul-sucking Big Pharma (sales, marketing, and training, now recovered, thank you), I started my blog, RachelintheOC back wow, in '08. Mostly because like you, I had something to say. I embraced blogging and social media like a dog to a bone. Blogger, Facebook, Twitter — yea! Okay…I'm here everyone. Now what? *crickets*

Perhaps many of you feel the same. And *that's* where I come in. Utilizing my almost two decades of sales, marketing, and training, plus my own experiences in social media and publishing, I learned how to brand myself, what pre-release activities work prior to book launch, all about Amazon, and what it takes to make my four books (***Broken Places, Broken Pieces,** A Walk In The Snark, and The Mancode: Exposed*) Number One bestsellers.

I own BadRedhead Media, creating effective social media and book marketing campaigns for authors. My articles appear regularly in *The Huffington Post, Feminine Collective, Indie Reader, OnMogul, Transformation Is Real, Blue Ink Review, Book Machine,* and several others.

I started this challenge to give you the best tips I've learned over my ten+ years in blogging and publishing, and to help you take advantage of what I've learned since I started my professional career in sales and marketing back in 1987. *Much* has changed, of course, but I learned so much about how to treat people, what works, and what doesn't. I apply those principles daily connecting with readers, bloggers, reviewers, influencers, and to continue to establish not only my brand as an author, but also as a businessperson with my own clients. Learn all about me here: BadRedheadMedia.com

It's important to note that if you are marketing a book, this challenge takes into account that your book is well-written, professionally edited, formatted, and designed. This challenge will *not* address the writing aspects of your book, except to say that a poorly written book packaged and marketed beautifully is still a poorly written book. Readers are discriminating and will crucify you in reviews. If your writing is not at the level it needs to be, take your time to make it exceptional.

If you haven't published yet, this challenge is perfect for setting up your author platform and pre-marketing your work. If you aren't an author and have no plans to be, cool. Take these tips for your blogging platform or small business.

Each day, I will assign you one tip (minimum), as well as the reasoning behind it, examples, visuals, the how-to, and the links. Do as much or as little as you want. Some will be more challenging for you, some brain-dead easy. My goal is to help as many people as possible in various stages of experience. If you still are confused after an assignment, Google for more info, go to the sites I mention directly, click on the many, *many* links I provide, or try YouTube for tutorials. The truth is out there.

Let's do this thingy.

I

WEEK ONE

DAY ONE: LET'S TALK TWITTER

If you don't have an account, you need one. Why? You might not like Twitter much (though I personally think it's great), but guess what? Your *readers* are looking for awesome book recs there. They talk to each other, participate in Twitter chats (more on that later), and love to interact with their favorite authors. Plus (and it's a *big* plus), *Google indexes tweets now* -- that's good news for your SEO (Search Engine Optimization).

Go to Twitter.com and see if the name you want is available. You have *fifteen spaces total* for your handle (aka, username). Preferably, use your name, or add author to the front or back. I don't recommend your book's title, because in all likelihood you'll be writing more than one book, and then what? Start smart: *use your name* or some iteration thereof. This also goes to personal branding: we brand the author, not the book.

A new update: you now have fifty spaces for your display name. DO utilize *the new option* to lengthen your display name (and you can even add hashtags or emojis), though I'd avoid getting too cutesy.

As you can see in my example below, I added #BookMarketing and Consultant to my display name. This helps people identify me as a person, not simply a business name. The hashtag makes me visible in Search (I tested it and yes, I do come up in a People search).

> **Rachel Thompson, #BookMarketing Consultant** ✓
>
> @BadRedheadMedia
>
> aka #author @RachelintheOC. Social strategist. Founder #MondayBlogs, #BookMarketingChat, @NaNoProMo! Motto: #WriteWhatScaresYou BadRedheadMedia.com
>
> ◎ Helping you help your damn self since 2011
>
> ℘ bit.ly/30DayBMChallen...
>
> ▦ Joined February 2012

Unsure how to use Twitter at all? Start with their <u>Help Section</u>. It's quite robust.

Twitter is a great channel for networking and visibility, for connecting with readers, book bloggers, reviewers, and other publications who can help publicize your book; it also can send a huge amount of traffic to your website and blog. It's not, however, all that great for sales.

> *Tip*: Don't be that person who auto-DMs (sends an automated direct message) people with a 'Hey, thanks for the follow! Go buy my book! And review it! And tell all your friends!' because that's not only annoying, you will lose followers before you even have them. In fact, the new Twitter Safety update on the Twitter Rules for spam warns people about autoDMs, and is actively suspending accounts of people who do.

(If you have an auto-thank you in place, go disable it right now, especially if you're using TrueTwit -- a bot to confirm whether your followers are bots? Just no.) To disable, go into Settings > Apps > and Disable any apps that you've given permission to that might be auto-tweeting on your behalf. And, done.

Assignment: If you don't have an account, sign up now. If you do, let's optimize your bio! Click on your little face in the upper right-hand corner. It says: View Profile >> Click. On the right >> click Edit Profile. This is where you type in any changes to your bio. When done, remember to save.

You only have 160 characters for the bio *including spaces* and now 50 spaces for your display name, so make them count. You need your bio to achieve three main goals:

- Have a shortened, customized link (I recommend bit.ly) to your book (I suggest linking to Amazon, as they are the largest online retailer), or blog or business, if you're not an author.

- Describe who you are and what you do in an interesting way, with a *verb*
- Be found more easily in Search by using hashtags (which create a hyperlink)

Take a look at my author bio here: http://twitter.com/RachelintheOC and use it as a template for your own. Go ahead, steal my ideas.

Here are a few additional insider tips:

- You only have 160 characters for the bio, right? Leave enough room to *add an additional website* (shorten using a link shortener). See how there are two websites in my bio? One goes to Amazon, and one goes to my author website. Got room? Add a third.

- If you have more than one Twitter stream (as I do, since I'm also @BadRedheadMedia), be sure to add the @ symbol, which creates a *hyperlink*. If you write for a site, or are affiliated in some way with a publication or a business, do the same thing.
- Location is *only* important if you're a local business looking for local customers. Use that space to write more copy. I share a statement *(Share your story. You matter.)* You can put whatever you want.
- Use a high-resolution picture for your avatar and graphics header. Mike Parkinson from *Billion Dollar Graphics* suggests that "humans process images and numbers close to 60,000 times faster than we process words" (Source: Canva). If your visuals are blurry, potential followers will pass.

Twitter is an important book marketing tool because it's *where many of your readers are.* Remember, book marketing isn't about your comfort, it's about *book discovery.*

See you tomorrow.

DAY TWO: VERBING YOUR BIO AND PINNING A TWEET

Yesterday, we optimized our Twitter bio. How did that go? I'd like to discuss today a few points I mentioned in more detail:

- "Verbing" your bio
- Pinning a tweet

Verbing your Bio

What does it mean to 'verb' your bio? It's a funny way to word it, I realize, but it works. When we write (or even verbalize) our typical bios, authors say, "I'm an author. I write books -- mysteries, non-fiction, sci-fi about blue bunnies who eat green cheese." Whatever.

Instead, try writing it this way: "I'm a memoirist whose books *inspire* childhood sexual abuse survivors." Or, "I write travel books to *embolden* agoraphobics to leave their homes and see the world." For Twitter, you need to shorten that up, of course, so edit, edit, edit.

How can you **verb** your writing? Does it inspire, teach, scare? What does your writing *do* for people? In other words, how do you want your reader to *feel* after reading your book? Put *that* in your bio. Create *action* and a sense of movement.

* You can use this tip with *any* bio, by the way.

Pinning a Tweet

Twitter offers you the option now of *pinning* a tweet to the top of your timeline. I recommend pinning your most popular tweet *or*, if you have shared a somewhat non-annoying "Buy my book!" tweet, you can share it there -- though remember, if you've added your book link to your bio (as I mentioned in yesterday's post), you won't need to do that spammy stuff.

Tip: Sometimes it's helpful to have a tweet at the top to make it easy for people to purchase your books, particularly if you're running some kind of short-term promo.

If you look at my screenshot from yesterday (or simply go to my Twitter author profile now), you'll see that I have a pin from Pinterest there -- it's by far my most popular tweet ever -- retweeted over THREE THOUSAND times as of this writing. It represents my brand, genre, and advocacy, so I keep it there.

To pin a tweet: Click on the **More** button (the ellipsis icon located below each tweet), and click on **Pin to your profile page**. That's it. *Note:* you can only pin your own tweets, not a retweet or someone else's tweet.

Also, you can change out your pinned tweet anytime -- for example, your most popular blog post, most retweeted tweet, latest book promo, or link to your book. You can now even pin a tweet from Twitter's mobile app (on iOS and Android).

Assignment:

- Head on over to your own Twitter stream and pin a tweet. Click on your own timeline, find a tweet you like, and pin it. Easy peasy. Don't like what you pinned? Pin something else.
- When you're done with that, go into your bio and *verb it up*. Save your changes. Remember, if you don't like the verb you picked, you can always change it.

See you tomorrow.

DAY THREE: "TWITTER DOESN'T APPLY TO ME" -- WRONG

I hear from some writers, and even top experts, who say what I'm recommending with regard to Twitter utilization doesn't apply to fiction authors, and I couldn't disagree more. These tips work *regardless* of what you write. Readers are on Twitter and they are looking for great reads, regardless of genre; so are book bloggers, book reviewers, book clubs, and more.

(Several of my BadRedhead Media clients are top New York Times bestselling authors -- fiction *and* nonfiction. The marketing, social media concepts, and branding strategies are the same, regardless of genre. Remember, *we brand the author, not the book.*)

Here's the issue: most newbie writers join Twitter and start following primarily only other writers. Their stream then becomes filled with authors hawking books, so they become disillusioned with all the book spam, blaming Twitter *for their own mistake*. Um...

Targeting

As writers, bloggers, authors, and small business people, *we need to be strategic* with Twitter and follow our ideal customers. Are your ideal customers or your ideal readers more authors? No. Then why are you following so many?

Yes, I believe we form and join communities to support each other and that's great. Do that, but don't *exclusively* do that. See the difference?

Assignment:

- Find your ideal readers on Twitter by strategically targeting them using ManageFlitter. I use the Pro plan because I manage over 20 accounts, but you can start with the limited free plan. (I do recommend using the full-featured Pro plan for only $12/month, but that's your call.) There are other options out there and that's fine -- just be sure they don't require any kind of 'auto' welcome messages because those are annoying, e.g.., "Welcome to my Twitter! Please follow me on Facebook, buy my book!" (Again, Twitter is cracking down on this so hopefully, that junk is not a requirement anymore. We shall see.) Blech.
- Many people mistakenly believe they are stuck at following 5,000 people. *Totally false.* They simply are not *managing* their followers properly. Once

<u>you hit 5,000</u>, Twitter imposes a 10% ratio limit, where you cannot follow 10% more than is following you (sorry, math). This is why you must manage your followers (using a program like ManageFlitter); start dumping the blank profiles, non-follow backs, and inactives, which are preventing you from growing.

- Growth is important, because you want to reach your ideal readers, interact, and connect. It doesn't matter from a 'Oh, I have to have a HUGE following,' perspective because that's not completely true. It matters from the 'I have an engaged, targeted following and we are connected,' perspective.

- Use keywords like *#bookblogger, #bookclub, #bookreviewer* in either the Account Search or Tweet Search option (another reason why you want to use hashtags in your bio). For readers, use your genre. Also, input the handles of writers in similar genres and follow their followers. You can also look at their public Lists and poach from there (more on Lists, later).

- Can't afford a paid tool? Use Twitter's free Search. Twitter also has a fabulous and under-utilized <u>Advanced Search</u> option.

Tomorrow we'll discuss what to tweet about.

See you then.

DAY FOUR: WHAT TO TWEET ABOUT, THE NEW 280 CHARACTER COUNT, CURATING CONTENT

Many people are unsure what to tweet about (or post on any social media channel in general), because it feels unnatural, and forced -- which is why authors end up hawking their books constantly, or small businesses only discuss selling their services. ME, ME, ME.

NO, NO, NO.

This is a mistake. If you were at a dinner party or say, in line at the movies, what would you discuss with the person next to you? Likely, not your book or service (one would hope). You'd discuss topics that interest you, a news story, something you have some kind of expertise in.

Twitter is no different. Pick four to five topics of interest, and find articles, quotes, pictures, and share blog posts (yours and others) to share around those topics -- mix in occasional tweets about your own books, your own blog posts, or something promotional *occasionally*, and then it's not as annoying, obnoxious, or uncomfortable.

Listen, self-promotion, even the selling situation itself, is unnatural. We all recognize that it's forced. How can you make it less uncomfortable? Make it less about ME, ME, ME, and more about common interests. Connecting with others is about finding common ground, right? *Listen as much, if not more, than you talk.*

The New 280 Update

You now have 280 characters to tweet, not just 140. Do you have to use all 280? Nope. Twitter, at its best, is short and pithy. If you choose to utilize all 280 characters however, be *strategic*. Here are my tips:

- Longer quotes (always give attribution!). If you're quoting someone with a Twitter account, be sure to tag their @ handle (e.g., @BadRedheadMedia)
- Multiple links in tweets (but don't go overboard). I recommend no more than two or your tweet looks too cluttered (and remember to shorten those links)
- Create a theme and share multiple tips on that one theme
- Create a list post

Curating Content

Unsure how to find what to tweet about? Here's how to find articles:

- *Content*: If you use <u>Hootsuite</u> (which I *love* -- more on that tomorrow), pay for the Pro version, and add in many of their free (or paid, up to you) content apps, like Right Relevance, UpContent, or FlipBoard.

- Try new PromoRepublic -- they are like Hootsuite, Buffer, and Canva all wrapped up in one. At only $15/month, that's far less expensive than having all three. (Disclosure: this is an affiliate link.)
- *Free option*: set up Google Alerts. You can receive these as often as you wish (hourly, daily, weekly, etc.), on any number of topics and is easily editable.
- *Quotes*: I find most of my quotes in either Pinterest or Goodreads as a jumping off point, usually by entering keywords. So, for example, I'll look for quotes about say, courage or focus (whatever word I'm rocking at that time), and see what comes up. (I'm very careful to make sure the quote *always* has attribution -- not a fan of unknown quotes, generic sayings, or B.S. 'inspirational' crap.) We'll discuss more how to create visual quotes in future challenges.
- Buzzfeed, Upworthy, A+, Mashable, etc., are all great sites for popular, trending, daily content.
- News aggregators like Flipboard and Scoop.it are both free, easy to use content curation options that will help you find great articles about topics that interest you and your readers -- remember, it's not all about you and your book -- it's about connecting.
- For more literary content, I adore Maria Popova's Brain Pickings. Lots of unique finds.
- Read more about content marketing here.

Assignment:

- Either create Google Alerts on at least three of your topics of interest OR
- Create a free Flipboard or Scoop.it account. Once you've done that, we'll discuss sharing it tomorrow (or dive in and share it yourself right now).
- There are many new tools coming out daily. Here's a <u>great list from Buffer</u> for finding great content and managing it all.
- Try Hootsuite, Buffer, or PromoRepublic. They all have free options. **You can do it.**

That's it for today. Change your paradigm if you think your content is only about you. Twitter (or any other social media channel) is about providing interesting content, interaction, and listening more than you speak. *Engagement is key.* Our optimization from the last two days should do our selling for us.

See you tomorrow...

DAY FIVE: HOW OFTEN TO TWEET AND HOW TO SCHEDULE

Today we're going to discuss social media management tools. Most people new to social media log in and out of Twitter, Facebook, and maybe Instagram or Pinterest on and off throughout the day and guess what? That's fun and all, but it's a huge-ass time waster. What if everything you needed to check was all in one place?

Well, it is. (Er, mostly.)

I've been a fan of Hootsuite for many years now. I know, I know, there are many Tweetdeck fans out there and I tried it, *I did*. But I just don't like the format plus, I incorporate so many other social channels into my dashboard, like G+, LinkedIn, etc., and Tweetdeck doesn't allow for that so...if you're willing to find out about other social media management tools, let's move on...

1) **Hootsuite**: The free plan allows you to have 3 free profiles, which is plenty to start out. Add in Twitter, your Facebook page and/or personal account (more on the difference next week), and G+, LinkedIn, or Instagram. The main reason I really like Hootsuite is because you can schedule in your tweets and shares *as well as* still interact with people, all in one place. (Yes, they have a mobile version which sadly, I don't love). They used to have a suggested content option which was great. I'm not sure why they ditched it, but you can use many free apps mentioned previously to find content. Their blog is also the bomb and they often have free kickass webinars, too.

2) **Buffer:** I adore the Buffer people, and their blog is *amazing*. Their free plan is limited (you can only schedule in 10 tweets at a time), but hey, it's enough to give it a try and see if you like it. The Awesome plan is only $10.00/month, so pretty afford-able, and best of all, their free mobile app is terrific. I use it a lot on the go.

Sadly, you can't interact with followers using Buffer -- it's strictly a scheduling tool only, and they no longer have a 'sug-gested content' component, which sucks. However, they have added a 'content inbox' which allows you to add RSS feeds of your favorite sites, so that's a cool addition.

Now you can see why I have both tools. There are a few tools out there that do *everything*, like SocialBro, Klout, Sprout Social and Post Planner -- all are great if a little spendy. If you have the means and time, check them out. In fact, I've been giving Social Pilot a chance lately and I find them easy to use for scheduling in content (both online and mobile) as well as reasonably priced.

3) Another great option is **CoSchedule** (they have terrific **free templates** to organize your social media scheduling, blog calendar, etc., so if nothing else, go look at all their free resources.)

4) **Klout** This used to be simply a way to score others and receive perks. Now it's a scheduling tool also. I haven't used it only because I've found my groove with other tools. If you use it and love it, great.

5) Did you check out **ManageFlitter** yesterday? If so, and you upgraded to the *Business* plan ($49/month), go click on Engagement >> Suggested Content and then pick from a myriad of topics -- it's awesome. (No, they're not paying me to say this stuff.)

 If you stick with the more reasonably priced *Pro* plan (which I use), you can still use the *PowerPost* option, which allows you to share tweets, FB shares, and LinkedIn posts *right there from ManageFlitter* -- they even figure out your most optimal times. Kinda cool.

6) Try out **PromoRepublic:** if you think you need a degree in graphic design, think again. This site has readymade pro graphics where you can simply add your book cover or logo. Try it.

So, go. Pick one of those social media tools mentioned above, create an account, and start using it. Should take you all of ten minutes to set up and try it out. ***That's your assignment.***

How often to tweet?

People ask me this a lot, and really that's a personal choice, though I'll share my schedule with you. In general, my advice is to spread out your tweets, rather than doing the 'check in, tweet dump, check out' which is likely what most of you are doing now, especially if you only tweet from mobile.. *I see you nodding.*

Many people are opposed to *automation*, preferring instead for pure organic tweeting. This is an old argument, that's been circulating since I started on Twitter in 2009. With tools like Hootsuite, *you can do both*. If you schedule in a blog post, then discuss it organically when people kindly retweet (RT) it, or you RT theirs, it's a nice, big, tasty soup.

For my author account, I schedule in tweets on Hootsuite *every four to five hours* (depending on the day), leaving room for live tweeting, RTs, etc., in between. Here's a screenshot of my Hoot schedule for a typical day (I schedule about a week in advance):

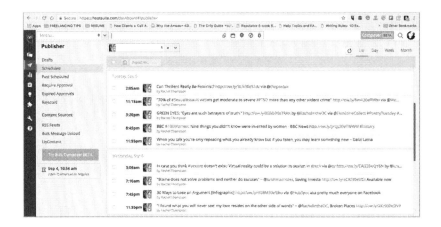

How long does this take me to schedule? Maybe 20-30 minutes at night, when it's quiet and the kids are in bed. (By the way, I like this horizontal LIST format. It works with my brain. If you prefer, you can choose a daily, weekly, or monthly calendar format.)

If you're always on the go and don't have that kind of 'sitting down time,' I recommend using Buffer. Here's a screenie of that:

This is the web version. Again, I prefer their mobile version, which pretty much looks the same. Go give it a try. Their analytics are easy to access which is a great benefit -- see which posts resonated the most, and reschedule them in again at a later date with one click.

See you tomorrow, challengers.

DAY SIX: RELEVANCE AND MEANING OF HASHTAGS (#MONDAYBLOGS) AND CHATS, VISUALS

Kind of a lot today, but you're smart. You got this.

I find that people new to Twitter (or social media in general) ignore hashtags completely, as if they don't exist, kind of like your annoying little brother. If you ignore that thing, it will just go away, right? Wrong.

1) Hashtags: Hashtags are an incredibly useful tool and despite the literary bobbleheads who feel they are ruining classic lit somehow *scratches head,* I'll explain how you can use them easily on every platform, as hashtags have now taken over the world like a virus -- but in a good way (okay, that sounded funny, but just go with it).

Definition: A hashtag is any word or phrase immediately preceded by the # symbol. When you click on a hashtag, you'll see other Tweets containing the same keyword or topic (Source: Twitter). This is why it's SO important to have a few hashtags in your bio, and to use them in tweets. However, you do not want to go overboard either.

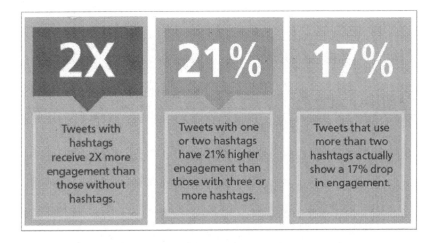

(Source: LinchPinSEO)

History (if you care): The first time a # was used was to organize an event -- a way to help people connect using Twitter. #Barcamp, back in August of 2007.

Memes and Chats: Both memes (rhymes with themes) and chats use hashtags. The difference is that a meme is what you'll see say, in what's trending on Twitter, whereas a chat occurs at a specific time (usually once a week).

A personal meme example: I wanted to create a way for writers and bloggers to share our writing that's *not* book related -- I got tired of all the book hawking, so I created #MondayBlogs in 2012. Share your blog posts, any blog posts, whenever it's Monday where you are. It's grown so much, it trends nationally now each week. The only rules are:

- it can't be about book promotion (your book is on a blog tour, free today, on sale, whatever). NO book promo.
- No porn or nakey pictures, because really? (tasteful erotica, fine, *as long as it's a blog post*)
- blog posts only, not quotes or random thoughts
- we ask you RT (retweet) others

Tip: Schedule in your #MondayBlogs posts using Hootsuite, PromoRepublic, or Buffer! See how easy that is? Bit of planning comes in handy. Once you get used to participating, you'll be shocked at how many new followers you'll get, as well as the amount of website traffic you'll receive on Mondays. I typically receive four times my usual website traffic on Mondays, for comparison.

Now, between 10,000 to 20,000 people participate weekly. Jump in any week, just by using the hashtag. Post your blog whenever, any day, as you usually do. Just *share* on Mondays using that hashtag. Read more here. I retweet as many people as I can from the @MondayBlogs stream (we are limited to 1,000 RT/hour), and we do not guarantee RTs for that reason, but we do our best.

Chats: If you jump into a chat, be sure to pay attention to the chat topic and be respectful. I recommend using Tweetchat.com or Twubs.com to participate in chats (enter the hashtag once, and then it does it for you from there on out). Here's a great list of Twitter chats on my blog, but you can also Google it to find more.

Mistakes: The biggest mistake I see authors make is referring to their own book with a hashtag in a way that nobody else will understand or recognize, e.g., #BlueBunnyTriology, which isn't something people typically search. ***Think like a reader*** -- use a hashtag like #SciFi or #Paranormal instead. Creating a new hashtag nobody recognizes or uses doesn't help you in terms of visibility.

Caveat: You *can* add on to a known hashtag since the first part of the hashtag will already come up in search, e.g., #Caturday-Funny instead of just #Caturday. Make sense?

More: For a complete rundown of hashtags, read this great article on Social Media Examiner. It's worth noting that all social media channels picked up on hashtags by 2013, and you can use them in your shares (particularly on Instagram), which creates a *search hyperlink*. Helpful for your visibility. Again, don't go overboard.

2) **Visuals:** Tweets and shares with images receive 18% more clickthroughs, 89% more favorites, and 150% more Retweets than tweets without (Source: Hubspot).

I'm not a graphic artist *and* I'm super busy, so I needed to find an easy, quick way to create visuals. I was thrilled when I discovered Buffer's visual creation tool, Pablo. Choose from over 600,000 royalty-free images (many from Unsplash.com, my favorite royalty-free image site -- gorgeous photos). I also like PromoRepublic's easy tool, since many of the graphics are pre-made and I can simply add my book cover or logo. Some people prefer Canva, which is also a great tool.

Enter a quote, play with some fonts, even add your cover art (as a 'logo') if you want (if sharing your own prose), and then either share via Twitter, Facebook, Pinterest, Instagram, or schedule into Buffer if you have an account, or download and share via Hootsuite or another social media management tool.

Takes seriously, maybe a minute or two to do all of that. See the one I created below. I timed it -- two minutes.

Assignment:

- Go look up what's trending on Twitter. It's always

in the upper left if you're on the Notifications page. Sometimes there's a fun meme, like what day it is, e.g., as I write this, it's #LaborDay. See what people are saying and jump in, if appropriate OR

- Find a Twitter chat on the list I provided and participate by typing in the hashtag. Remember, most are weekly.

- Go to Pablo by Buffer (it's free and you don't even need an account), and create a visual. It will take two minutes, and then share it on one or all of your social media channels. Create a quote, quote me, quote yourself (from your book or blog), quote your favorite author in the world, whatever. Whatever you do, *always give attribution.*

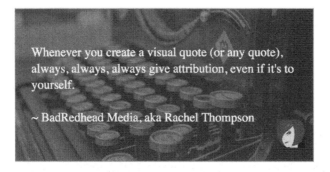

Whenever you create a visual quote (or any quote), always, always, always give attribution, even if it's to yourself.

~ BadRedhead Media, aka Rachel Thompson

Tip: sometimes, memes are well, kind of ridiculous, and a lot of the tweets somehow become political or religious (and even downright racist). Unless your book is political or religious, I recommend avoiding those topics, if possible. Are politics or religion your brand? Great. Speak on, fellow writers.

Otherwise, avoid. Honestly, #Dogs can be trending and someone will make it about politics. Trolls come out from under the bridge when these topics come up, and you risk alienating readers completely. Do what's best for you.

See you tomorrow, challengers.

DAY SEVEN: WEEKLY WRAP-UP (TWITTER ANALYTICS, TRAFFIC TO WEBSITE, READ MY BLOG)

W ow, it's been a week -- is your brain full yet? Lots left to do, so I'll make today fairly easy, plus it's Sunday, and who wants to work on a Sunday, right?

Ironically, Sundays are my busiest day, writing and scheduling in for #MondayBlogs, reading and researching.

Tip: I also set aside time to research, learn, and catch up -- so let's get you in the same habit. Here's a wonderful list of top blogs to do that:

Assignment:

- List.ly top social media blogs -- learn, read, research.

This was mostly, but not solely, a week about Twitter -- if you gave up, go back through days 3-6 to learn what you missed. Some people get Twitter, some don't. ***Don't give up.*** Remember, it's important to connect with readers (and not spam them constantly). ***If you want to learn more about Twitter, keep an eye out for my 30-day Twitter challenge coming next year.***

THE most important point to remember about Twitter and why you need it as part of your book marketing platform (besides connecting with readers): *Google indexes tweets, so from an SEO (search engine optimization) perspective, Twitter carries more weight than Facebook, which is likely where you spend most of your time.* More on that this coming week.

I wasn't able to cover everything, and there's *a lot.* New Twitter changes are always afoot, so we'll be able to cover those at that time. If there's anything you can count on with social media, it's that it changes...constantly. Tip: visit Twitter's blog occasionally to see what's new. In fact, by the time you read this, there will already be more changes.

Finally, between starting this challenge and writing this book, both @RachelintheOC and @BadRedheadMedia have been verified by Twitter. Twitter used to have a mysterious process to verify accounts (usually reserved only for celebs, famous authors, musicians and such), but now the rest of us can request verification. Head over to this form in Twitter Help to learn more how to go about it however, for now (as of this writing), verifications are on hold. Check in often to see how Twitter decides to update this process.

Assignment:

- Go into their **Help Section** and type in any questions you may have. The best feature is Twitter Lists. Learn more here. Also, you can tweet @Support and they answer -- really. How cool is that?
- Here are ALL the articles on my BadRedheadMedia.com site about Twitter. Hope they help.

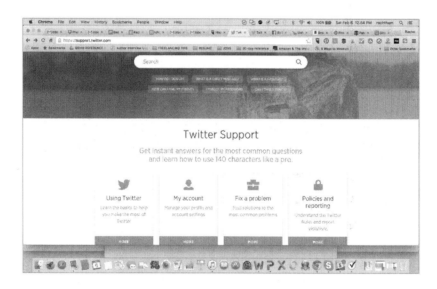

Enjoy your day and I'll see you tomorrow, when we'll tackle Facebook.

II

WEEK TWO

DAY EIGHT: FACEBOOK PERSONAL ACCOUNT VS. AUTHOR PAGE/CREATING A PAGE

F acebook is a two-fold way to build relationships: via your personal 'friends' account and via an author *Page*, where people *Like* stuff — no 'friending' required. I'm constantly surprised at the amount of authors who either don't have an author page at all, or don't even know they need to have one.

According to Facebook's legal terms (which we all agree to when we open our account), <u>Section 4, point 4</u>:

You will not use your personal timeline primarily for your own commercial gain, and will use a Facebook Page for such purposes.

You can do so much more with a Facebook page than with your personal friends account anyway. Besides, who wants to be constantly 'selling' to friends and family? Meh. Don't be that person.

Also, for SEO purposes on Google, your *page* will show up, not your personal 'friends' account (and definitely not anything you post -- probably a blessing for most people), so it's important you put that you are an author, not a book, not a public figure, or a community page. We are marketing you as an *author*. (If you are a blogger or business person, choose that option.)

Here's how to choose or change that: >>> go to the About Section, and click on Category. Hover to the right and an Edit button pops up. Click on it and pick which category you desire.

Assignment:

- If you don't already have a Facebook page, go create one now. You want an author page, *not* a book page. Again, *we brand the author, not the book*. You'll write more books, so why create more work for yourself when your next book comes out?

I'll give you more tips as we go along this week how to flesh it out. For now, just create the darn thing.

- Already have a Facebook page? Great, here's an **insider tip:** click on your header (the graphic at the top of the page). Have you added any information there, e.g., how people can find you? Probably not. Click the *edit* button, and add in *all* your formatted links, e.g., Twitter should read http://twitter.com/RachelintheOC so it hyperlinks.

Here's a screenshot of my Rachel Thompson, Author Facebook page (any likes appreciated) header with formatted links:

I typically add in all my social media channels, website, and Amazon (or other online retailers), links for my author newsletter, anywhere people can find me. Be sure to click 'Save' when done.

See you tomorrow.

DAY NINE: CREATING PAGE TABS USING FREE WOOBOX

I t took me *forever* to figure out a way to add tabs to my Facebook page -- you know the thingies where you can add in your Twitter, Pinterest, Instagram, newsletter, etc. Maybe you had it all figured out, or you have no clue what I'm talking about, but I wanted a *free* way to connect my other social media channels in a cool, easy manner.

Here's a visual so you know what I'm talking about. Look at **the column running down the left side:**

How could I create those darn tabs? I asked people, I searched in Facebook Help everywhere, I Googled, and nothing. Finally, the heavens parted and I discovered free Woobox.

Assignment:

- *Go, my challengers, go.* It's free (though they offer a paid version which *you do not need*); log in with your Facebook account, and click on *Static Tabs*.

With the free version, you can add in your Twitter, Pinterest, YouTube, and Instagram accounts. Just copy and paste the URLs (minus the twitter.com or YouTube.com part etc., which they've already provided for you), and you're golden.

Here's what it looks like in Woobox once you've added all your tabs. To check, go over to your Facebook page (remember, this is *not* for your personal account):

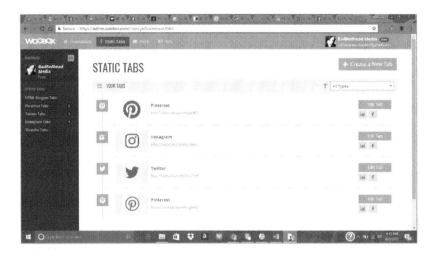

Why do this at all? Some readers never leave Facebook, particularly the older demographic, so you can run your platform all from your page (not that I recommend that's *all* you do -- Facebook owns your Facebook page, not you, and as mentioned previously, Google doesn't index Facebook Page posts with anywhere near the same credit as they do Twitter, Google+, YouTube, etc.).

This does help people find you more easily on other social channels; you're saving them from having to look for you.

- Once you've added the tabs, click on the *More* tab and scroll down to *Manage Tabs* -- reorder the tabs however you want.

Assignment #2:

- Another cool free app: **Freebooksy** offers a free author marketing app for authors on Amazon. It's easy to import to your Facebook page. <u>Read all about it here</u> and honestly, it's super easy.

If you want to get fancy and know HTML, you can do fun things like change the font, add bold and italics and stuff. Otherwise, ignore those options. If you get stuck, go to <u>Freebooksy</u>'s site for help. They really are awesome. Be sure to update it as you release new books, change publishers, or update pricing.

Click on <u>my page</u> to see what the app looks like here.

See you tomorrow.

DAY TEN: USING NOTES ON BOTH PERSONAL AND PAGES

D id you ever notice that you have a **Notes** option on both your Personal account *and* your Page (well, if you didn't have a Page until yesterday, you probably didn't know, but anyway...). Notes are a wonderful way to share a bit of your writing, blog posts, guest blogs, etc., without it being spammy, which if you don't know by now = *bad*. Think of Notes as sticky posts, if you will.

Let's discuss Notes on your personal 'friends' account first. The way it works is the same as on your Page, but you'll need to remember to *avoid including a link to your books* because of that *Facebook rule* about not promoting or personal gain with your personal account, remember? I know.

Assignment 1: Notes on your Personal Account

- Go to your personal account, click on the *Add Apps*

under the More tab. Then click on Add the Notes tab, click on Add Note.

- Once you click on Add Note, you'll see this:

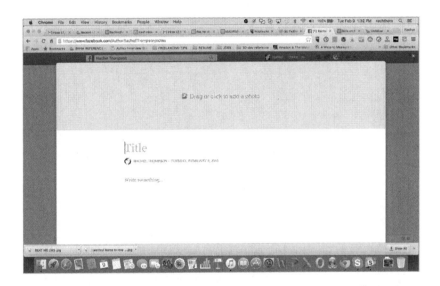

- It's pretty self-explanatory from there. Drop in a photo, copy and paste your copy (or write something original). Make sure you save your work, as you would in any doc.
- I use royalty-free photos from Unsplash.com (as mentioned in previous assignments), but you can pull from whatever royalty-free site you want. *Note: be sure to add a copyright notice at the bottom, and I also recommend adding a 'this post/article originally appeared on wherever' line as well, if recycling content.

- *Only share content you have rights to.* If you're not sure, ask the owner of the site where it originally appeared, or skip it if you're uncomfortable. I typically share my own blog posts, or excerpts from an upcoming work as a way to tease it out, aka pre-marketing.

Here is what my **Personal Notes** looks like:

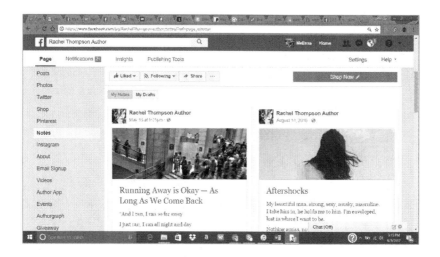

Cool, right? What's even better -- once you hit publish, it automatically shows up on your wall and all the Like, Share, etc., buttons show up at the bottom of the Note, so it's easy for people to see what you've shared, the comments, and they can share as well. Remember, *no links to your books*, but it's okay to share to your website.

If you find a typo or want to fix or update a note, you can always go in and *edit*, too.

This is my most popular note: see it here *if* we're friends -- see, that's the issue with Personal Notes -- only your 'friends' can see them: https://www.facebook.com/notes/rachel-thompson/weve-lived-in-shame-long-enough/1068072763226665 *which is why you want to create the same Note over on your Author Page.*

Assignment 2: Notes on your Page

- *Create a Note* on your Author Page. Same process, except go ahead and add the link to your books on Amazon, B&N, or wherever else you want people to purchase them. Add your website, Twitter, whatever, too (again, update as needed).
- *Share this note* on your other social media, e.g.., take that URL *and create a tweet/share out of it* using Hootsuite, or Buffer, or whatever social media tool you're using. Here's an example:

Cracks by Rachel Thompson, Author @RachelintheOC http://ow.ly/Y8Umm BROKEN PLACES #relationships

---

- The only difference between Personal Notes and Page Notes is in the information Facebook provides to you: they tell you how many 'reads' you've received on each Note, which is kind of cool:

That's it for today. Hope you find Notes helpful.

See you tomorrow…

DAY ELEVEN: MORE FACEBOOK PAGE TIPS AND TRICKS, WHEN TO POST

Messaging vs. Share

When you first create your Facebook Page, you have the option to either receive private messages OR make your page Shareable. Unless you want even more PMs (private messages) from strangers you don't know, change that from messaging to share.

Note: Facebook has added the ability for you to answer messages using AI (artificial intelligence) bots. If you want to employ these, you'll need to leave the messages option active.

Assignment 1:

- Click on the Settings tab >>> scroll down to
  Messages >>> click on the Edit button. *Uncheck* the
  box that says, "Allow people to contact my page
  privately by showing the Message button," >>>
  click Save Changes.

Once you've done that, go look at your page. Now your page
has a **Share** button.

And there it is.

When to Post

Ask any author when the best time is to post to on Facebook and they'll look at you like you have two heads. They have NO idea. *All the time? When I have time? When Mercury is in retrograde?* are typical answers.

Well, not exactly.

According to research:

The best time to post on Facebook is 3:00 p.m. on Wednesday. Other optimal times include 12:00–1:00 p.m. on Saturdays and Sundays and 1:00–4:00 p.m. on Thursdays and Fridays. (These are EST.)

*Engagement rates are **18% higher** on Thursdays and Fridays, and weekdays from 1:00–4:00 p.m. tend to see the highest clickthrough rates. On Fridays, Facebook use spikes by 10%. Since people tend to be happier on Fridays, Neil Patel* *suggests posting funny or upbeat content to match your audience's mood. All times are EST. (Source: Hubspot, 2016)*

Got all that?

Another fun fact:

80% of the U.S. population lives in the Eastern and Central time zones combined. (Source: KISSmetrics) so if you, like me, live on the West Coast, schedule your tweets and shares to start going out *early,* long before you're even awake.

What does this mean for us as authors? Using our social media scheduling tools like Hootsuite or Buffer to schedule in content that fits with these times is the best plan.

Assignment #2:

- Schedule in a post to go out at 2am pst, 5am est. Also, schedule something funny for Friday afternoon est. Come on, you can totally do this. (If you're just diametrically opposed to funny, find a great quote instead.)

If you're stuck on where to find content, remember, I gave you options in previous assignments. All the tools are there -- now use them. (Okay, okay: Pablo by Buffer and Pinterest are great places to start.)

Assignment #3:

- Just a few clicks -- if you don't mind. Be sure to give my Facebook pages a like -- and hey, *a share* -- if you haven't done so -- I appreciate it.

https://www.facebook.com/RachelThompsonauthor
https://www.facebook.com/BadRedheadMedia
https://www.facebook.com/BookMarketingChat

See you tomorrow.

DAY TWELVE: YOUR FB PAGE NAME (GET RID OF THE NUMBERS), CTA BUTTON, PINNING A POST

W anted to share this first: a really interesting article about your personal account's newsfeed from Hubspot -- and how to change what you might hate about it since people whine about the newsfeed frequently. You have the power to change it.

Today, I'm going to show you how to **personalize** your Facebook page URL. When you first opened your account, you probably didn't notice but the URL (in the bar at the top) has a bunch of numbers. When people ask for your Page URL, you don't want it to show those numbers, you want it to show your Page *name*. Much more professional.

Assignment #1:

- Go into the About tab (not Settings), and you'll see where it says Name. Hover to the right where it says Edit, and enter the name of the Page you want. I recommend your name and Author, e.g.., mine is Rachel Thompson Author (no commas). See below:

As you can see above, I already have my name, so Facebook is asking if I want to *change* my name (which I don't). You're only allowed *one name change*, so don't make the change until you are sure and ready. Typically, you cannot personalize your page name until you have something like 50 Likes, so don't freak out if you can't do this right away.

If you're still confused, visit this <u>username page on Facebook</u> for more info. Once you've saved those changes, your URL should no longer have numbers, only your name.

(Note: You can always start a new page, and merge the old into the new -- remember, nothing is ever set in stone with social media.) Many authors create pages with their book title -- don't do that. What happens when you write the next book, and the next? You only need ONE author page.

If you have created other pages, don't delete them! Merge them into your author page. *A note on merging pages: If you choose to merge two or more pages, FB will automatically merge whichever page has the *least* likes into the page with the *most* likes, so be 100% sure that you have chosen correctly. *There is no do-over.*

Verifying a Page

Many people ask how Facebook gave me that blue verification mark on my Author Page. Simple, I asked (well, I filled out a form). You can, too, though I'll warn you, just because you ask doesn't mean you'll receive in this case. They look at a number of factors: your entire social media platform, how many books you've published, your Google ranking, places you've published online, how interactive you are, etc.

You also *must* provide a jpg or png of either your birth certificate or your current driver's license. If you're uncomfortable doing that, then forget it. Those are your only options. Note: You can ask to verify your Personal account instead. They will not verify both your Page *and* Personal account. It's one *or* the other.

Here's the <u>link to the verification form</u>. Request to verify an account | Facebook Help Center.

Assignment #2:

- Right below your page header on the right in blue, you have a CTA (Call to Action) button. Click on it and create some sort of CTA -- if you have a book out, use the *Shop Now* button, and insert your Amazon URL. If you don't have a book out and want to drive traffic to your blog or business, use one of the other buttons (i.e., *Book Now, Contact Us, Sign Up*, etc.).

You can change out your CTA button at any time. For example, when I was looking for sign-ups for this challenge, I changed it to 'Sign Up' and included the link to my sign-up form on my **BadRedhead Media** page. Now that the sign-up period has closed, I've changed it back to 'Shop Now.' For my author page, I have a 'Shop Now' button.

Assignment #3:

Just like with Twitter, you have the option to pin a post to the top of your Page (you cannot do this on your Personal account). I typically will pin a promotion, event, or my latest blog or featured guest post.

- Go to your Page. Choose whatever post you feel is most important for people to see right away. To pin (or unpin), simply hover over the gray arrow on the top right of that post and click 'pin post.' It's *that* easy.
- If you want to boost that post (e.g., pay for it to show up in people's newsfeeds), you'll need to add your credit card info. You can boost a post for as little as $5 to $10. *This is not an assignment -- simply pointing out the option.*

This is our last Facebook post. I hope you've found these tips helpful. I wrote a post based on my observations so far. I'd appreciate any shares if you're so inclined:

This Is The Reason Your #Author Platform Impacts Book Sales http://ow.ly/iKzv302jVHP by @BadRedheadMedia

See you tomorrow.

DAY THIRTEEN: MARKETING PLANS: WHAT THEY ARE, WHY YOU NEED ONE

L et's move on to marketing our books. Finally.
Many authors are kind of terrified of that M word -- *what if I don't know what marketing is? I don't have a business degree. Aren't marketing and branding just fancy buzzwords, anyway?*

I seriously hear (and read) this daily. Truth is, you're already likely marketing your books without even realizing it. Marketing is really just a way to get the word out about your books, whether that's through advertising, social media, blogging, simply talking about them with people (or getting them to talk with each other -- e.g.., word of mouth), newsletters, etc., and it's been around for hundreds of years.

When you look at *all* the various ways we have available to us to market, some of us 'turtle,' as my teen daughter refers to it when she becomes overwhelmed, and I love that description. I call it 'buzzy brain,' where everything is buzzing at me: do this, do that, get this done, get that done -- ack. Make it stop.

This is where the marketing plan comes in. It's really just a way to tell all these buzzy things to get out of our heads, and write that ish down (sorry, teen talk). So, let's do that.

Assignment #1:

There are many great blank marketing plan templates available free online. Here's a great site with a free blank plan, and some tips to get your started: AllIndieWriters.com.

I also like to share Joanna Penn's free, award-winning marketing plan so you can see what she did for her book. It's completely filled out. Sometimes, seeing what somebody has successfully done is also helpful.

- Download a blank template and peruse Joanna's as well. Fill out as much as you can. If you already have a marketing plan, actually *look* at your plan, read it, study it, and discuss it with your book manager (if you have one) or your cat. Too many authors take zero responsibility with their own book marketing and *that is why they fail*. Remember, publishing is a business, and businesses need a plan.

Assignment #2:

Take a look at these fabulous resources. Unsure of who your demographic is? Most authors are. I know I had no idea with my first book -- um, women? Haha. I really had zero clue. Here are a few great resources to find out:

- <u>Pew Research Center</u> is a nonpartisan fact tank that provides tons of great info about our world. Enter whatever search terms you're looking for about demographics and it's likely in there. All free info.
- <u>Hubspot</u>: one of my favorite marketing blogs, hands down. If you know nothing about marketing, this is a great place to start. Their services aren't cheap, but *the blog is free.*
- <u>Buffer</u>: another favorite marketing and social media blog. Free, also.
- <u>CoSchedule</u>: a wonderful source of marketing statistics and planning. Highly recommended.

The best part about creating a marketing plan? It's free. Well, except for the time it takes for you to research and create it...but aren't *you and your work worth that time?*

Assignment #3:

Read this article by my fabulous former author assistant Melissa Flickinger which discusses many of the needed components of a book marketing plan -- all free, too:

How to Create and Market your Author Platform FREE
http://ow.ly/lns130eUf0O
   by @MelissaFlicks via @BadRedheadMedia

Ultimately, your book marketing is your responsibility, because only you can express the voice of your work, and only you can truly connect with your reader. As Patti Smith says:

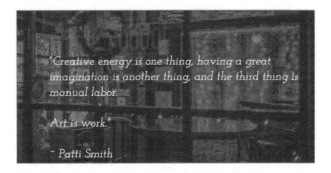

"Creative energy is one thing, having a great imagination is another thing, and the third thing is manual labor.

Art is work."

~ Patti Smith

See you tomorrow.

DAY FOURTEEN: GOOGLE +, WHAT'S GOOD CONTENT?, #MONDAYBLOGS

What is Google+?

W ell, it's controversial and a bit complicated to go into, so I'm not going to take the time, or your or my brain, to try to explain it all, so let's make it really simple: **Google owns it, so get thee there.** In fact, Google owns a staggering 65%-75% of all search engine market shares.

Yea, they're going through a lot of changes yada yada... whatever. Until that happens, you really don't need to do more than post there daily (using the social media management tool of your choice **makes it easy**), follow a few people, and share or +1 a few posts if you feel like it. Don't really worry too much about growth for now.

For your SEO, *it matters.*
Read THIS:

*Google+ posts are crawled and indexed. This is a **huge** advantage, especially when you consider that the privacy settings and data sharing restrictions on Facebook and Twitter posts mean that the vast majority of them **will never been indexed at all.** This means that when it comes to Google+ marketing, posts on that platform have the ability to build PageRank, while posts on other social media sites are lost forever in the ether. (Source: ContentFac.com)*

Here's more:

Content that you post to Google+ is far more likely to show up in search results than other pages, websites, articles, and content posted to other social networks because Google ranks their own social network higher and they crawl it faster. The added benefit is that Google even previews certain Google+ posts with rich snippets (profile picture, media, etc.), giving them even more real estate in a search. (Source: Buffer).

Assignment #1:

- Create a Google+ brand page (like on Facebook, you need an Author page; on G+ you need a brand page). It's not the most user-friendly platform and if you have trouble, keep at it. It took me awhile to figure it out. Google has plenty of helpful info to walk you through how to create your brand page (tip: you *do not* want a business page).

If for *no* other reason than your G+ page will integrate with Hootsuite or Buffer, and your posts will show up in Google, ***do it.*** Goodness, do people whine about this. Re-read the paragraphs above, do the research, and then just do it. Additionally, here are some **tips** on how to increase your visibility from the Social Media Examiner.

G+ has made it much easier to create a brand page than before. Once you create your personal account (just like in Facebook), **click on Brand on the bottom left,** and create your page. Note: You do not need a Business page (a common mistake writers make -- unless you are a brick and mortar business selling products or services), create a ***brand*** page.

Step 1:

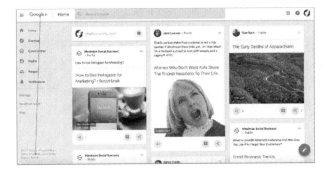

Click on 'Brand' on the bottom left.

Step 2:

Click on the BIG RED BUTTON 'Create Google+ Page'

Step 3:

Create your Brand Account Name (I recommend keeping it consistent with your Facebook Page name, e.g., Rachel Thompson, Author).

Boom. Done.

(If you still can't figure it out, go back and try again, google it, or go their Help Section linked above.)

Blog Content

Most authors write about writing. *Snore*. Who is your audience? Other writers? **Not usually**. You want to connect with readers. You may need to rethink your content strategy. Write about your interests and your authenticity will shine through.

A few ways to see how your blog/website is doing? I mean, *really* doing?

Assignment #2:

- Install Google Analytics on your site. How many views do you get? Many people are disappointed they don't receive many comments, but comments aren't a true indicator of views or shares (or your SEO).
- Check your Alexa Ranking (***scroll down*** to type in your URL -- or any URL for that matter). You *do not need to pay for Alexa* if you do exactly as I say here -- ***scroll down to enter your URL***. They also have a handy, free browser extension I use constantly -- again, free. The lower the number, the better you're doing.

As for what makes for 'good content?' Think back to your keywords we discussed earlier in the challenge. What are your main topics of interest? For me, I'm passionate about (on my author blog): *sexual abuse, relationships, love, loss, surviving trauma, women's issues* -- so those are the topics I write about.

These all tie into my books in a way, but not in a direct, 'hard, sell, buy my book!' kind of way.

I read an article recently by a top blogger who shunned the idea of 'good content,' and said, *'write whatever you feel like -- whatever comes to mind! however often you want or don't want! make it organic!'* and I about fell over.

Any top marketer will tell you to have a plan, and work the plan. Blog *at least* once weekly, whatever day works for you, and share it on Mondays using the #MondayBlogs hashtag (remember, you can schedule in your blog post tweets and shares using your social media management tool).

Branding is really about creating expectations for your reader. If I write about my typical topics, and then throw in a post about oh, woodcarving, then I'm totally off-brand, and my readers will be checking to see if they're in the right place (or if I've hit my head on some wood). Be consistent.

Assignment #3:

- Post a blog post this week at some point, and schedule in some tweets and shares for #MondayBlogs -- remember, we only share on Mondays, and *no* book promo. Here's an example of my some past tweets for #MondayBlogs. Feel free to copy the format:

*How to Fix Your Disorganized #Writing Life by
@KW_Writes via @BadRedheadMedia
http://ow.ly/Yim4n #MondayBlogs #authors*

*Note: this is for my biz blog and my audience is authors

*#Twitter Guide for Writers: The Ultimate DO's and
DON'Ts http://ow.ly/LNhj30g6h1E by
@BadRedheadMedia #MondayBlogs*

See you tomorrow.

III

WEEK THREE

DAY FIFTEEN: IDEAS FOR YOUR MARKETING PLAN -- LET'S GET SPECIFIC

Promotions

One of the best ways to let people know about your book is to **not** *talk about it yourself, but to let readers know about it in other ways, and get them talking.*

For all of you who are constantly tweeting and sharing, "Buy my book!" links, this will probably be pretty eye-opening. I rarely share a 'Hey, go buy my book!' tweet.

Instead I do things like:

BargainBooksy.com: There are many pricey promotional sites which offer newsletters that go out to large databases of eBook readers — I like this one because it's affordable, they have a large base broken out by genre (in my case, nonfiction), and they are very easy to work with. Their Nonfiction list goes out to 85,100 readers and the price is $25.00. This site only works if you're planning to discount your book, or if your book is already priced between .99 and $5. Caveat: you can only book one promo with them every 30 days.

If I have a few free days, I will pay for a FreeBooksy instead, which goes out to 99,000 (Nonfiction) readers and costs $75.00.

There are many, many more promotional sites I use and recommend because they go directly to your readers, people you may never be able to reach on your own. I like to use *BookMarketingTools.com* (you pay $29.00 to reach 25+ sites after filling out **one** form) if my book is going free.

Discounting books: my normal eBook price for *Broken Places* is $4.99, but I've recently re-published so I have the book on sale for $2.99. I made sure to list my book with as many promotional newsletters as budget allowed -- creating buzz is so important. I've found that constant "My book is on sale!" tweets aren't an effective selling tool (shocker), so paying for promotional newsletters with large subscriber lists is a good workaround.

Assignment #1:

- Go to *BargainBooksy* and/or *FreeBooksy* and at least *look* at their promotional options. ***NOTE: I do not in any way guarantee you any kind of results if you book a promotion, nor am I affiliated with them in any way. If you have other programs you prefer, by all means, use them and let me know about them.***
- If you want to check out a bazillion other sites first, head over to Reedsy for a look at their free book promotion database. It's vetted and updated constantly. Very cool.

Author Platform

Making a name for myself: this is important for any writer, particularly nonfiction authors. Some online publications pay, some don't. I didn't trip over the *Huffington Post**, *Indie-Reader, Feminine Collective, The Good Men Project, Transformation Is Real, Book Machine, Blue Ink Reviews, Amazon Author Insights*, and others. I didn't ask for any favors — I used my own blog over *many* years to establish my expertise (why are you still not blogging again?), and then I pitched them. Sometimes they came to me.

I've had my fair share of rejections, too (*Elephant Journal* has zero interest in my stories of survival and recovery from childhood sexual abuse, so see? It happens to me, too.).

*Huffington Post has now opened up to everyone, and you

no longer have to pitch them. My cats can write for them now. Google is not indexing the blog posts, however, so the exposure component is questionable.

You need to decide for yourself if you will only write for sites that pay — that's your call. I wrote free for many years, and still do for some sites because it often leads to something else (e.g., inclusion in anthologies that pay out in royalties). Now, I write mostly for pay. Regardless, the exposure helps your visibility, reader base, and most importantly, your SEO.

Guest blogging, podcasts, and interviews: give and receive. I often have people guest post for me and vice versa. This is totally free, and if you're not doing it, you're missing out on a huge visibility opp. Look for bloggers with whom you have similar interests and approach them. This is the *building relationships* I speak so much of. You blog for them and find new readers; they blog for you and find new readers. Win/win.

Keep in mind: to attract high profile guests and influencers to your blog, they will check your Alexa ranking, website ranking, social media proof, and website optimization to see if it's worth their while. The onus is on you to make guest posting on your blog an attractive prospect. Respect their time.

Same goes for podcasts and interviews. Podcasts are popular and here to stay. Join groups with authors and bloggers who write what you write, and invite them to write for you (if you're not a podcaster) in exchange for an interview. As always, be polite and use your inside voice.

Here are a few of my recent guest podcasts: <u>Robert Stern</u>, <u>Blondie and the Brit</u>, <u>Why I Social</u>, and <u>Alexa Bigwarfe</u>.

Assignment #2:

- Admire a blogger or writer? *Go visit their blog and see if they have guest post guidelines.* Ask if you can submit a blog to them *or,* invite them to write for you! Don't be upset if they reject you. Many top authors are quite busy and unavailable for guest blogs, but may be open to having you write for them.

Tip: Always edit your posts thoroughly before submitting, include a high-resolution author pic, book cover .jpg, and all your links. Better yet, create a media kit (you can see my media kit here). Be the professional you are.

Generosity: One of the reasons I offer challenges with info like this, created #MondayBlogs, #SexAbuseChat, and #BookMarketingChat, is to give back to others. It's not complicated, all that time-consuming (okay, total lie) or difficult, and the rewards are immense: people engage with me on a much deeper level than if I simply spam a link at them, or beg them to read my work. I'm giving opportunities and ideas with no expectation of anything in return.

*What can **you** offer to others?*

Further research*:* Is your book not selling at all? There has to be a reason. What are you doing? What are you *not* doing? How professional is your book? Did you slap together a few sentences and upload it to Amazon?

Here's an *excellent article by Joanna Penn* that covers many reasons why that may be happening. Perfecting your book marketing doesn't happen overnight. Take your time, create a plan, work your plan.

See you tomorrow.

DAY SIXTEEN: WHY BETA READERS AND ARC READERS MATTER AS PART OF YOUR MARKETING PLAN

How many of you actively utilize beta readers *before* your book comes out? As a newbie, I wasn't really even sure what beta readers were, and certainly not how to make the most of their marketing potential. Let's define and discuss.

What's a Beta reader?

Let's first define *what a beta reader is not*. A beta is not:

- an editor
- a critique partner or group (though they can be)
- someone you pay for professional services

A beta reader *is*:

- a peer or interested reader who has some knowledge of grammar, spelling, and what makes a good story (fiction or nonfiction)
- is interested in helping you, but will be honest about what works, or doesn't work, with your manuscript
- someone who understands the publishing process and what the beta reading process is all about.

Many authors are terrified of showing anyone their work and this is a huge mistake. *Ginormous*. Why? What do you think is going to happen when your book is released? Yea, reviews. And then what? You are at the mercy of the buying public, and they can be brutal.

**Utilizing beta readers helps you responsibly handle any issues prior to release
to make your book the absolute best it can be.**

How to Find Beta Readers

Remember how I keep saying that social media isn't that effective for sales, but awesome for networking and building relationships? *This* is one of those reasons. Social media is a terrific way to find your beta readers. I can't tell you how many people begged to read *Broken Places* long before I ever released it. (and I'm already taking names for *Broken People* -- are you interested? Let me know) Join my Street Team.

I've found Twitter and Facebook to be particularly helpful in this regard. How specifically? Make it *clear, simple, state the title, topic, and how to reach you.* Here's an example tweet:

Looking for #betareaders for my next book BROKEN PEOPLE out in 2018.
Interested? DM me. #memoir #sexualabuse #relationships

(Don't do this if you're not prepared to be serious about it. Stay in contact with these folks. People who are willing to sacrifice their time for you will be mighty ticked off if you don't let them know when the beta is ready for review.)

Assignment #1:

- Create a beta reading document (wherever -- Word, Google, on your refrigerator). Create at least three tweets, three Facebook shares, a list to store names, as well as a goal date -- when do you plan to have betas read your book?

Which leads to our next point...

When Should I Have Betas Read My Book?

Your betas are still readers, and many of them *can* be influential, so *do not give them a first draft.* (I refer to my first draft as 'word vomit,' so as you can imagine, nobody sees that POS but me and my cats -- and they're not even not happy about it.) Give them as decent a final draft as possible, but it doesn't have to be perfect.

Some writers choose to send out their entire manuscript (aka MS), some only the first 100 pages, some send chapter by chapter. Some writers wait until their book is entirely finished and is going into final edits, others wait until after editing to send out a more perfect copy. Some writers are terrified that beta readers will download the unfinished MS to piracy sites and claim it as their own (which can be solved by stamping a copyright watermark on each page).

Honestly, here's my feeling: we can sit inside our bubbles and never share anything, ever, for fear that others will steal our intellectual property, or we can copyright as we normally would, and go on about our day. It's up to you.

Assignment #2:

- *Send your book to some beta readers and start getting feedback.* Here's the thing: don't just randomly start sending out emails to strangers or DMing/PMing people you don't know -- select people who have expressed interest in your writing.

or

- If you're not ready to do that, start working *today* on building those relationships, writer friends.

You may not be at the stage for beta readers...yet. **But you will be.** Decide how much of your book you'd like betas to read, at which stage, and how many betas you want to show it to. Stephen King suggests sending it to ten people you really trust. In my own experience, I usually send beta copies to between twenty to thirty people. I'll tell you why below.

For specifics on the type of feedback and how to send out your work, here's a great article from The Book Designer. Some authors ask extensive questions of their beta readers -- I usually keep it pretty simple: *what works, what doesn't, give specifics.* Remember, your betas are real people with real jobs and real lives, too. Note: many beta readers will simply proof-read I've found (which is great -- the more eyes on it, the better). However, you typically want more than that. You have an editor. *Let them know this.*

Here's a great list of questions from <u>Fiction University</u>, though I caution you not to go overboard and ask your betas to answer *all* of these or you'll scare them off.

The Marketing Side of Beta readers

Once you have feedback back from your betas, now is the time for the follow up -- you want to politely thank them for their time and effort (etiquette, people -- write thank you notes/emails), and be sure to ask *politely* for a review when the book goes live on both Amazon and Goodreads.

Tip: don't hound them if they don't post their review -- again, real people, real lives. True story: I've witnessed some pretty nasty posts and emails from authors to beta readers who didn't get their reviews up, and here's my advice on that: **don't do that.** Be the bigger person here. Beta readers are often influential readers, reviewers, and bloggers, who talk to each other, especially about authors behaving badly. Don't be that author.

Most beta readers are happy to comply with writing a review for you. When your book does go live, you want to immediately send a special 'heads up' email to your betas that the book is up and could they please go and write their reviews right away. And here's why 25-30 beta readers: you want at least ten reviews to go up the day you release the book, and twenty-five within the first week, *if possible*. Sending the book out to people who are already fans of your work means they are more inclined to help you reach that goal. Why? The more reviews, the more comfortable potential readers are in buying a new work.

Post a follow up email to remind them the book is live, and could they possibly get their reviews in. Again, don't be a pushy douchenozzle about it.

One final note: an ARC is an Advanced Review Copy, which is completely different. An ARC is the completely edited, ready to go version of your book that you send to reviewers and book bloggers free of charge in exchange for a review. Also a helpful way to obtain reviews.

Still unclear on the difference between beta readers and ARC readers? Here's a great article about it.

Hope you find this helpful. See you tomorrow...

DAY SEVENTEEN: IT'S THE LITTLE THINGS

Today is about giving you some overall everyday tips I find useful. There are several assignments. Do two, do all -- it's up to you. Some of it reviews what we've gone over in case you cheated a little bit on the hard stuff.

Here we go:

Google+ Pages: Yes, there's a difference between a personal account and a *brand page* (and they even now have business pages, which you don't need unless you have a physical brick and mortar business). No, I cannot walk you through all the steps (there are A LOT of you).

I *can* tell you that you need to have:

- a gmail (aka email) account first (even if you never freakin' use it),
- then create a personal G+ account,
- then create a brand page.

That's the process, and it's kind of annoying, but very easy. Either manage your brand page directly on your desktop or mobile, or loop it into your social media management tool. Hootsuite and Buffer previously only integrated with brand pages, though now you can add both personal and brand. I personally only integrate my brand page.

Assignment #1:

- Here's the link in the Help Section to get you started. Google+ is a pain in the arse to set up but you can do it, and it is important for your SEO and Google ranking.

Twitter: You will not gain more followers on Twitter *unless you follow people.* It's really *that* simple. If you sit and wait for people to find you, you'll be sitting and waiting a long time. One author told me she waited three months for one new follower and she was so happy. That boggles my mind -- no waiting necessary.

We discussed using ManageFlitter, which I love, but there are plenty of other following/unfollowing apps out there. You do not need a huge following; you need an *engaged* following of readers, book bloggers, book reviewers, and other author supporters.

Assignment #2:

- Take 10 minutes every day and follow 50 people to 250 people (if your account is small, go with 50) using *keywords*; unfollow people who haven't followed you back after (however many) days -- I give them 20-30. It seriously takes that minute amount of time. If you can be on Facebook posting cat pictures or asking me how to find more followers on Twitter, you can follow people on Twitter. You *have* the time.

Marketing Plans: I'm lucky to have a terrific author assistant who is efficient and affordable. Delegation is important when you can't do it all, especially the little admin stuff that drives me insane. If you think I'm busy, she runs circles around me.

Assignment #3: Please follow her on Twitter here: http://twitter.com/TheRuralVA. Emilie assists me each week during #BookMarketingChat as well.

New Stuff:

Email signature: Are you using your email to take advantage of potential readers? Many authors do not, and you're missing out on a wonderful passive selling opportunity. Here's a screenshot of my email signature on my personal account:

Warmly,

Rachel

Award-winning bestsellers *Broken Places*, and *Broken Pieces*
and the newly released *BadRedhead Media 30-Day Book Marketing Challenge*

Founder, BadRedhead Media
Media consultant, Social strategist
creator #MondayBlogs #SexAbuseChat and #BookMarketingChat on Twitter.

Social Media Director, Authorbytes

You should follow me on Twitter here - @RachelintheOC and @BadRedheadMedia
Facebook Pinterest LinkedIn Instagram

Websites: RachelintheOC.com and BadRedheadMedia.com

I provide all the links to my various books, websites, and social media, and other pertinent info.

Another cool free email signature tool is WiseStamp, which allows you to use icons to create your signature. Very cool as well.

Assignment #4:

- Create *some kind of email signature* that includes links to your social media, website, and at least one book (if you have one).

Medium.com

Have you considered publishing your blog content on *Medium*? It's a wonderful platform started by those cagey, smart Twitter guys, and it has millions of readers. It's surprisingly easy to use, integrates with your Twitter account, and is one more way to connect with readers.

I find it incredibly easy to build a following there: I'm already up to 7.2K followers, which shocks the you know what out of me since I've only been on there since May, 2015. It's worth noting, I post blogs frequently (mostly reposts from my own blogs), comment, and follow people. I also pitched a few of their publications and several came to me asking me to write for them, which increases visibility exponentially.

*They now have a $5/month fee but that's not required and I don't pay it. Also, you can write *original* articles for them and get paid per click. It's a great way to develop a following if you don't have the energy to do the whole website/blog thing. Kind of like having a built-in audience.

For a full run-down, here's a great article from the Social Media Examiner.

Assignment #5:

- Sign into Medium and create an account, and at
least look around. You simply have to use your
Twitter credentials, and they do the rest for you.
Here's me: https://medium.com/@RachelintheOC
and if you follow me, I'll follow you back. I
promise, you'll find it super easy.

See you tomorrow.

DAY EIGHTEEN: AMAZON TIPS YOU NEED TO KNOW NOW

When Amazon stated they were going to pull peer reviews (and actually started doing exactly that), authors wondered: *how on earth would Amazon know how/if I know another author? It must be through social media, right? So, I'll pull all my social media links off my Author Central Page (more on that below), and that will solve the issue, right?* Wrong.

There's a theory that you are likely the culprit of how Amazon knows who knows whom, and I'll show you exactly how...and you'll be kicking yourself that you didn't figure this out earlier because it's so obvious. *I'll state here and now that this is a **theory**, and I'm sharing what's out there -- and while it may or may not be true, here's how I'm avoiding any issues.*

Searching for Your Own Book and Then Sharing the URL

When you head over to Amazon to search for your own book, or even Google, Amazon supposedly is able to *track* the results of that search. So, let's say I go to Google and search for *Broken Pieces by Rachel Thompson on Amazon*, the URL at the top of the Amazon page looks like this:

My Book/ref=tmm_p

See all that stuff in italics (starting with /ref) at the end? That's information Amazon, it is said, uses to determine where the search originated from. I'm not a techie person at all, and I'm not a coder (so for you coders out there, you could probably explain this a lot better). When you then share this entire code (including the end coding), you are sharing where and when the search originated -- with you. If you then shorten that code and share it on your profiles, every time someone clicks on that code, Amazon tracks it back to *you.*

Or this is total B.S. and you're laughing at how dumb this is. Regardless, people worry about this so I wanted to include it to make you aware.

Point is, anytime you share your Amazon URL, you only need to share *up to* the ASIN number

(the part highlighted in blue) -- that's IT

This time, let's do a search *inside* Amazon. *Broken Pieces by Rachel Thompson* looks like this in the URL:

My   Book/ref=tmm_pap_swatch_0?_encoding=UTF8&qid=1470177186&sr=8-7

Once again, all that code at the end (not in italics) is *supposedly* telling Amazon where and when the search originated. If you share this URL anywhere, it will, again supposedly, be tracked back to you. That's how Amazon is connecting the dots. So, only share the area in italics, up to the ASIN number.

Here are three resources you can read more about the Amazon ASIN shortening info. Believe it, don't believe, whatever. Ultimately, it's up to you to do what you feel is best for you. Again, if this is of a concern to you, the solution is to share only up to the ASIN number. I'm not here to debate whether or not Amazon is really doing this, as it's clearly controversial. I'm merely *presenting an option* that could help you avoid a situation that may or may not be an issue.

- Amazon Link Anatomy http://ow.ly/YuY48 #amazon via K-Lytics
- Another view: Amazon is not using incoming links for review removal: Amazon Reviews and Timestamps via @cjewel http://ow.ly/YxCps

---

Assignment #1:

- From now on, only share links up to the ASIN number if you're concerned. If you have shortened links and posted to your various social media, change them to reflect only up to the ASIN.

By the way, this is not cheating in any way, this is simply common sense.

Moving on.

Amazon Author Central

Many authors don't realize they need an *Author Page* inside Amazon (this appears right under the book title and is a clickable link), and the only way to get one is through *Amazon Author Central* which is available to *all* published authors. It's easy to create and offers you HTML coding also (i.e., bold, italics, etc.). You add your author bio, pic, link your blog, Twitter, and even a video trailer if you have one. Also, you can ask people to Follow your page.

---

*Important: You must create an author page for each country. Yea, I know, kinda sucks, but the author page does not automatically populate over to other countries.

Assignment #2:

- You can only create your own *Author Central* page if you have a book out. If you don't have an author page, go create one now. If you don't have a book out yet, add it to your *To Do List* for release.

Here's the About Author Central Page. You can take a look at my Author Page here (I only shared up to the ASIN by the way), and appreciate a follow if you please -- you must be signed in to follow me.

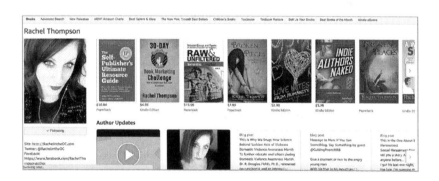

Amazon Giveaways

Did you know that you can run an Amazon Giveaway on your book? You can choose *either* print or eBook. There is no cost to set up the giveaway, Amazon does the work for you, and even ships the prize if you go with print (though you will pay for shipping) -- the only cost to you is to furnish the prize and shipping (in this case, the book). Giveaways are only open to the country in which you're a resident, e.g., I can only do Amazon U.S. For specifics, read the Amazon Giveaway FAQs.

I've done a few of these, and it's not a *huge, OMG, wow, amazing* way to sell a ton of books (it IS a giveaway, *give* being the key word here). However, if you tie it into your Twitter, you will see a nice bump in your followers which is cool, *and* you will increase your visibility. You can also require people follow you on Amazon (instead of Twitter), if you prefer.

Here's a screenshot of me setting up a giveaway for *Broken Places*, picking 5 winners of the paperback version at random, and requiring a Twitter follow:

Assignment #3:

Log onto Amazon and take a look at the Amazon Giveaway options for your book(s). The giveaway link is on *your book page (see screenshot below)*. Here's a <u>video</u> that explains how it works.

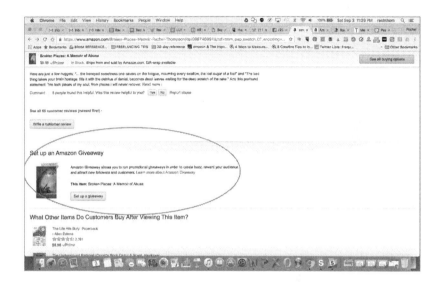

These are just a few ideas to help you make the most of Amazon.

See you tomorrow…

DAY NINETEEN: FREE BOOK BLOGGER REVIEWS, RESOURCES

How many of you know how to or are comfortable approaching book bloggers? Yea, that's what I thought. Not many. I wasn't either at first. It's kind of intimidating. *Who do you approach? How do you approach them? Why is it important? Where do you find them? When do you approach them?* Let's discuss.

*Note: I am discussing free book blogger sites.

Finding Book Bloggers

Assignment #1:

- Head over to this site and find five book bloggers in your genre. One of the best ways to find *free* book bloggers in your genre is to use

BookBloggerList.com, created by Barb
Drozdowich, author and book blogger herself. Barb
started the list a few years ago and it's been
approved by Publisher's Weekly as an outstanding
resource for authors.

Divided by genre and updated monthly, the list contains
thousands of active bloggers who review books. I know. I use
the list all the time for my books and author clients, and
it's great.

When should you ask a book blogger to review your book?

Assignment #2:
If your book is new (or if you're planning for your next
release), it's best to have an *action plan*:

- Put together a list of bloggers,
- Create a letter *politely* asking them to review your
  book with plenty of lead time (many book bloggers
  have a TBR pile -- to be read -- a mile high). Be
  sure to ask *how* they'd like to receive your book
  (Word, epub, PDF, Mobi). A few will only review in
  print, so obviously you'll have to wait until the
  book is released to send them a copy, or at least
  have a printed ARC to send.
- I recommend sending out a *personalized* query
  (more on that below) 8-12 weeks prior to release,
  one at a time.

- Send a short reminder a week before; however, a review from a top blogger is welcome at any time, even six months out.
- Do not mass email book bloggers (they hate that), or say 'Dear Book Blogger.' They hate that, too. Wouldn't you?
- Besides, mass unwanted emails violate the CAN-SPAM Act.

What do you say in your query?

Barb has an excellent series to help authors in working with book bloggers, and she gives you step-by-step instructions in writing your query here in *The Author's Guide to Working with Book Bloggers* ($3.99 on Amazon). If you don't want to purchase a book to learn how to do it, google 'how do I write a query for a book blogger review?' and see what comes up.

How do I find free book bloggers?

Assignment #3:

- Take a look at these resource sites and find 5 more book bloggers to send your book to. Here's a great list from YourWriterPlatform.com.

- The Book Blogger List – (as mentioned above) a database of book bloggers organized by genre of interest.
- YA Book Blog Directory – a listing of young adult book review blogs.
- Story Cartel – all books on Story Cartel are free in exchange for honest book reviews.
- Directory of Book Bloggers on Pinterest – a curated list of book bloggers using Pinterest by Mandy Boles.
- Kate Tilton's Book Bloggers – a smaller listing of book bloggers that provide reviews.
- The Indie View – huge listing of Indie reviewers.

(There are multiple paid review sites and you're certainly welcome to search for those on your own. As my goal is to keep this short and provide *reasonably priced or free* resources, I'm only looking at free sites today.)

Professional Behavior

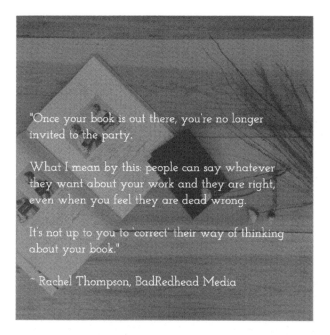

"Once your book is out there, you're no longer invited to the party.

What I mean by this: people can say whatever they want about your work and they are right, even when you feel they are dead wrong.

It's not up to you to 'correct' their way of thinking about your book."

~ Rachel Thompson, BadRedhead Media

Once your book is out there, you're no longer invited to the party. What I mean by this: people can say whatever they want about your work and they are right, even when you feel they are dead wrong. It's not up to you to 'correct' their way of thinking about your book.

We've all heard of 'authors behaving badly.' Don't be one of those authors.

That behavior haunts you for the rest of your career.

Too many authors forget they are selling a product, and the

reader is the customer buying that product. *Remember: the customer is always right.* Do not react to 1-star reviews. Do not get into arguments with readers, and especially with book bloggers. They are a tight-knit group and if you don't think they talk to each other and create blacklists, think again.

Change your paradigm: how about being grateful someone is reading your work? How about considering their 1-star review a win because you elicited such a strong emotional reaction?

Not everyone will love our work, and that's part of being a writer. Believe me, I had to learn the same lesson. Feel your feels -- we are human. Eat a gooey chocolate cookie, sulk in the bathtub, have a glass of wine. But then, as I coach my authors and clients, take all that angst that you would have put into replying to that reviewer, and put it into your work. You may end up with something amazing.

That's your tough love message for today.

See you tomorrow...

DAY TWENTY: PRE-MARKETING, WHAT IT IS AND WHY YOU NEED TO DO IT

M any authors are confused by the concept of marketing a product (their book) that doesn't exist yet, so they wait until after their book is out to market it, which is a huge mistake. Let's discuss.

According to <u>Seth Godin</u>, in a famous article he wrote about marketing advice for authors in 2006:

*"The best time to start promoting your book is **three years** before it comes out. Three years to build a reputation, build a permission asset, build a blog, build a following, build credibility and build the connections you'll need later."*

Can you imagine, three years? It's inconceivable.

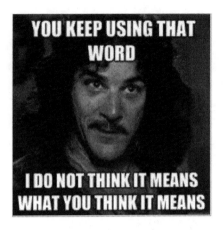

(Sorry, had to.)

When I first read that, I thought "Smart guy, outdated info." So wrong. I actually started pre-marketing my own first two books long before they ever came out. I began blogging in 2008, started Twitter and Facebook in 2009, released my two humor books in 2011, my *Broken* books in 2013 and 2015. By then, my reader base was firmly set.

What is Pre-Marketing?

Pre-marketing (aka, advanced book marketing aka, pre-selling) means developing relationships with readers, book bloggers, book reviewers, and other influencers via your blog, website, subscriber list, and social media by:

- providing interesting content and interaction,
- sharing teasers (e.g., visual quotes or excerpts), and
- generally increasing your overall web imprint *prior* to your book coming out.

The problem with waiting until *after* your book comes out?

It comes across as disingenuous to ask a total stranger to buy and review your book (e.g., those spammy autoDMs we all hate); if you've developed a months to year's-long relationship with a reader, blogger, or reviewer, they'll be much more inclined to help you out.

Assignment #1:

- Put together a pre-marketing plan if you don't have a book out yet, or if you have a new book coming out, create a plan for your next one. I recommend at least six months of pre-marketing, but work with what you've got.

Include in your plan:

- Blog topics (create an editorial calendar)
- Participate in #MondayBlogs
- Social media teasers, visuals, quotes of your upcoming work
- Excerpts on your blog, guest blogs, Notes on Facebook
- Time to grow your various channels
- Be *generous;* retweet/share, comment on others' blogs and posts without promoting yourself

Who's Your Demographic?
As we discussed previously, spamming anyone and

everyone to purchase your book is a big oops. Is everyone your demo? No. I know that my *Broken* books demo is primarily women, aged 18-50. That doesn't mean men ages 65 won't read my book, so I don't discount that opportunity or their opinions, but given that 1 in 4 girls is sexually abused, and I write about surviving sexual abuse...well, you do the math.

Godin also writes this:

"Don't try to sell your book to everyone. Consider the fact that among people even willing to buy a book, yours is just a tiny little needle in a very big haystack. Far better to obsess about a little subset of the market-- that subset that you have permission to talk with, that subset where you have credibility, and most important, that subset where people just can't live without your book."

According to the <u>Pew Research Center:</u>
As of January 2014, some 76% of American adults ages 18 and older said that they read at least one book in the past year. Almost seven in ten adults (69%) read a book in print in the past 12 months, while 28% read an e-book, and 14% listened to an audiobook.

Yes, those can be depressing statistics, I know. In a way, however, it helps us to narrow down who our subset of readers *really* is.

Assignment #2

- Nail down your keywords and demographic, so that you are spending your time growing your social media channels and marketing to the people who will be interested in your book when you release it. Remember, it's about quality, not quantity of followers.
- Go to the Pew Research Center and look up the topics you write about.
- Go into ManageFlitter and search on accounts and tweets that contain your keywords, and follow those people, as well as interact with them.
- Follow relevant blogs and,
- Leave comments on articles of your topics of interest.

Pre-marketing sets the foundation for marketing when you do release your book. To read more about the topic, visit my pre-marketing blog post here on BadRedheadMedia.com, or read this article on About.Money. This article on AllIndieWriters.com has a nice calendar to help you plan as well.

See you tomorrow.

DAY TWENTY ONE: KDP SELECT, TO FREE DAY OR NOT TO FREE DAY, WHAT'S A PROMOTIONAL NEWSLETTER

"My problem isn't piracy, it's obscurity, and free ebooks generate more sales than they displace."
~ Cory Doctorow

Once you publish on Amazon, you become far more aware of the various marketing options they offer (which you can certainly read about even before you publish -- and you probably want to, because they offer a lot of different options).

Some authors are adamantly against taking their books free, feeling that with all the effort, time, and money we put into our books, why would we want to give them away? Others feel that giving their book away free has great advantages, and are willing to use these options with great success. Let's discuss.

What is KDP Select?

KDP stands for *Kindle Direct Publishing* -- what all authors are part of if you have an eBook on Amazon. The KDP Select part is an exclusivity contract you agree to for a *three-month period* for your eBook version only, which allows you to take your book free for up to five days during that three-month period if you want to - not required. (Print and hardcover are not affected.)

You agree *not* to sell your eBook version on any other online retailer for three months in exchange for being able to *take it free* -- and no, you're not paid on free downloads. However, when you take your book free (depending on how many free downloads you have) once you cross back over to paid, your ranking will generally be much improved -- for a few days -- and that's where you can potentially make some bank.

If you choose not to go free, you have another option: the Kindle Countdown, whereby you can discount your book to say, 99c for one day, $1.99 the next day, and $2.99 the third day (this is just an example), all the while maintaining your normal royalty rate. There's also a dedicated website just for Kindle Countdown deals as well.

Kindle Unlimited is Amazon's subscription reading service, and if you're part of KDPS, your books are automatically part of KU. It will also automatically be enrolled in KOLL (Kindle Owner's Lending Library). Read all the details on Amazon here.

You can also now purchase advertising for your KDP books.

Assignment #1:

1. *Read all the Help articles I linked above.* Even if you're opposed to going free, you might learn something new, and consider the Countdown as a valuable option for your readers.

Personal experience: At one point, I had four of my five books enrolled in KDPS for this main reason: when I had them available on all the other platforms, 93% of my sales came from Amazon. I figured, why not put all my effort into sending people to Amazon, and take advantage of their merchandising ops when/if I go free?

I didn't take my books free every 90 days, nor did I do a Kindle Countdown deal but, when I did take them free, I went all out, creating a huge buzz.

(Why aren't I doing that now? New publisher, different strategy.)

Assignment #2:

What do I mean by *blow it up*? Even if your books go free, you still have to make the most of getting the word out there, aiming for as many downloads as possible. I use BookMarketingTools.com, pay the $29.00 to fill out one convenient form, and submit to about 30+ sites in 5 minutes (totally worth it). I also submit to *FreeBooksy, Digital Book Today*, and a few other sites here and there (paid options) I mentioned earlier (also linked on the BookMarketingTools site).

Again, if you use them, your mileage may vary and I am in no way associated with them. You may know of other sites that work better and if so, please share with me so I can include them in the next update of this book.

- Read more here: Here's my BadredheadMedia.com blog post with many different options, free and paid.

Many authors don't promote their free days because they see free downloads as missed sales opportunities, but I disagree. The visibility you are getting from the free downloads is something you would likely never get on your own; and remember, the more downloads you get, the higher your ranking and visibility when you cross back over to paid. *So, get out of your own way.*

Assignment #3:

Read these articles:

- Amazon's mysterious Sale Rank -- it's good info to read and absorb.
- Old study (2010) by Cory Doctorow, but still relevant on how free eBooks affect paid (especially print) sales.
- Great article on Medium about why top writers give away their work free.

What's A Promotional Newsletter?

We haven't discussed email marketing too much here, but I will say that it's a good idea to utilize an email marketing company like Mailchimp (the free option is fine) to at least start collecting names for an eventual newsletter. They will also stay within all the rules and regulations that can cause trouble for you if you were simply mass emailing people (a no-no). Read more on that here.

What does this have to do with going free or not? Well, if you decide to take your book free, or even discount your book, you can email your newsletter directly to people who have opted-in to find out about you and your book. These are readers who are interested in you, have signed up for updates, who want to know when your books are on sale.

Assignment #4:

- Make it easy for people to sign up for your newsletter. Add newsletter sign-up options to your website/blog (read the new Google pop-up rules so you're not penalized) and Facebook page.

Look at my BadRedheadMedia.com homepage:

Right there at the top is a sign-up form, but no matter what page people are on, that form is there. I use Wordpress.org, so that's a plug-in. Depending on which platform you use, you'll have to find out what's available for you.

Here's my Facebook Rachel Thompson, Author page (likes and shares appreciated):

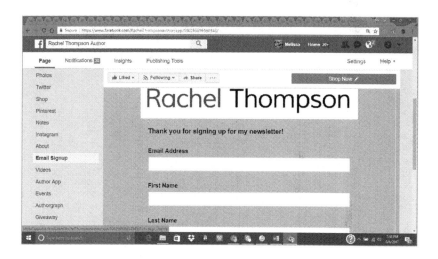

Again, easy for people to sign up. I use Mailchimp, so here's how they recommend doing it.

---

*Note: I don't recommend sending out newsletters

unless you have something going on, such as a new release, event, or promotion. People get enough email on the daily as it is.

BTW, if you're not following me on Twitter and Facebook, I'd really appreciate it.

http://twitter.com/RachelintheOC
http://twitter.com/BadRedheadMedia
https://www.facebook.com/RachelThompsonauthor
https://www.facebook.com/BadRedheadMedia

See you tomorrow.

IV

WEEK FOUR

DAY TWENTY TWO: IMPORTANCE OF A PROFESSIONAL WEBSITE, RANKING DATA, DOMAINS

Week Four, challengers. This is it...I hope you're still with me. This week is dedicated to *getting you polished.* Many of you likely already have a website or blog (I recommend a website with a blog), and might think, "Meh, what I have is okay." Ask yourself this: is "Meh" good enough?

Website Grader

How visible is your website? Have you done the SEO? Are your social media icons present and easy to find? Is your blog content (if you have any, but let's not go there today because I can't even with you if you don't) easily shareable?

Assignment #1:

- Your website is your home. It's all yours, and you own it (more on that below). This is where you invite people in to hang out, sit down, and chat for a while. *On a scale of 1 to 10, where would you grade your website right now?*

Assignment #2:

- Great. Now let's go over to the website grader site and see what you score *really* is: https://website.grader.com/ which takes about 30 seconds. Go. I'll wait.

Where'd you end up?

I got an 84 on http://RachelintheOC.com, and a 79 on http://BadRedheadMedia.com -- which doesn't surprise me, as we're in the middle of some upgrades.

If you didn't take the time to see your score (I mean, really? *Come on*), here's what the top of the report looks like:

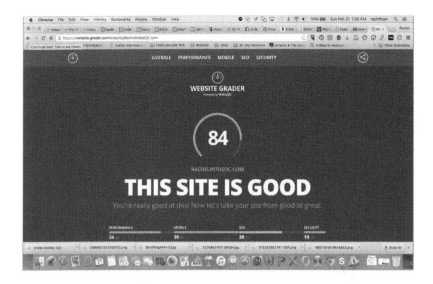

If you scroll down, you'll see a mobile score. If your site isn't mobile friendly, you definitely need to work on that (mine is 30/30 on both sites). They also give you suggestions on what to fix. All totally free of charge.

Alexa Ranking

Another important ranking factor that gives you insights into your analytics, visibility, sites linking in, etc. What is Alexa? Yet another company owned by Amazon!

Alexa Internet, Inc. is a California-based company that provides commercial web traffic data and analytics. It is a wholly owned subsidiary of Amazon.com. Founded as an independent company in 1996, Alexa was acquired by Amazon in 1999. (Source: Google)

I often use Alexa to check my own sites stats, as they do change. The goal is to have your site under 100K (for your country; I'm U.S.), if possible. Sites like Amazon and Facebook are generally top five.

Assignment #3:

* What's your Alexa Ranking? Let's find out. Go to Alexa.com and type in your website (remember, *scroll down* to find where to type your URL). Again, ignore having to sign up. It's free to do this.

Below are screenshots of my two sites using the Alexa Chrome Extension -- it shows my global rank, my US rank, and the number of sites linking in. This is especially important for book bloggers to look at -- if you site ranking is really high (bad), and you have less than ten sites linking in (bad), you have some work to do if your goal is to be part of a prestigious or large book tour company.

(I find most book bloggers are using Blogger, and are terrified to port their sites over to Wordpress, for fear of losing data. I was a Blogger fan, too, but found that my SEO sucked. Wordpress has a migration plug-in. I've used it twice now and while it's not perfect, it's been a fairly painless transition and I lost *nothing* because I backed up everything first.)

According to Bakerview Consulting's Bard Drozdowich, Wordpress.org (*not* .com) gets us the best Google rankings, and is also the easiest to work with now, with all the various shortcuts and plug-ins. I know that people have complained they need a degree in coding to run WP.org, but Barb will tell you she's not a coder and she recommend self-hosted Wordpress exclusively for all her clients (including me!).

(Barb is also a coach, so if you can't afford to hire her to design your site, she will coach you how to do it all yourself in her various blogs and books.)

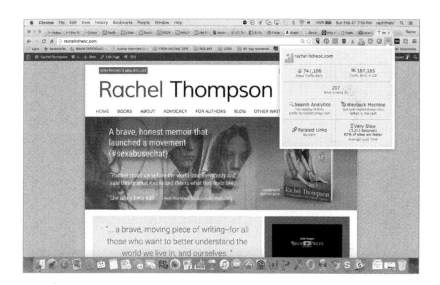

Assignment #4:

- Read: Here's an article she wrote for
  BadRedheadMedia.com with specifics on how you
  can use Wordpress, or switch to Wordpress.org from
  .com, and why it's the best choice for your author
  website.

Assignment #5:

- Speaking of which, register your damn domain,
  please. What do I mean by that? There's no reason
  your site needs to say
  RachelintheOC.com/wordpress.com
  or.blogspot.com -- it only costs you $10 to $12 or so

for the basic .com. If I'm speaking Greek here, read
this article on <u>PC World</u> about how to register a
domain.

This is probably the most important assignment of all.

I've given you a lot today. I hope you head hasn't exploded.
I'll just back out of the room now and go get some more
coffee.

See you tomorrow.

DAY TWENTY THREE: GOOGLE ANALYTICS, SEO (ALT TAGS, KEYWORDS, CATEGORIES), GRAPHICS

Let's do a little answering (kinda sorta) of your questions, first.

When I originally shared the last assignment in the free newsletter challenge, I was inundated with emails from authors and bloggers asking me how to improve their website grades and Alexa rankings. I'm not a website designer or Wordpress expert -- I know just enough to be dangerous. I can't solve all your individual issues (I'm not an SEO specialist or website builder), but at least now you know where you have to focus your efforts, right?

Resources: People I regularly recommend my clients to

- Bakerview Consulting's Barb Drozdowich
- Jah Kaine with Jerboa Design Studio

Also, people started freaking out about switching from free Blogger over to Wordpress.org, not so much because of the cost (it's not expensive), but because ***they're convinced they'll lose everything.*** I'm not sure why they think that -- did they Google it? No. Have you learned nothing from me in this challenge, people? Either research the plug-in in Google or Wordpress, or consult an expert. The sky isn't falling, I promise.

Here's a nice, easy, step-by-step guide to migrate your Blogger blog over to Wordpress. If you decide to do this and it doesn't work out, that's on you. As I said, I hired Barb to help me because she's very affordable and incredibly patient. If you don't want to do anything, don't. Up to you.

Google Analytics:

If you haven't downloaded free Google Analytics on your site, you need to. It's a great way to see what's really going on with regard to views, visits, and all those terms you might not understand but are certainly capable of figuring out, especially if you're on Blogger because their data is usually totally bogus. Here's a handy guide from ClickZ that breaks it all down.

If you're on Wordpress.org already, I recommend using the Jetpack plug-in as well as Google Analytics. You'll have a true picture of your visitors, views, and value (I just put that in for alliteration).

Assignment #1:

- Download Google Analytics for your site. They'll walk you through the steps. Check their Help Section if you get confused. Google stuff. You can even email them - they're very responsive.

Optimizing your blog posts

Some of you asked me why your site was rated so low. Consider these questions:

- How often do you blog?
- Are you using appropriate tags and categories for each post?
- Are you adding relevant keywords throughout your copy and in your headings and title?
- Are you adding alt-tags to each picture you share?
- Are you making sure the picture or links open in a new window?
- Offering a 'subscribe to my blog' link?
- Are your social media icons easily findable (top right is preferable)?
- Do you link to your own and others' content (inbound and outbound links)?
- Are you sharing your posts via social media?

If you're not sure what all this means, keep reading (and this explains your low website score). Well, at least partially.

Assignment #2:

- To learn SEO *basics*, read *The Free Beginner's Guide to SEO from Moz.* Hands down, the best guide out there. Every author needs to understand this stuff.

For more advanced tips, read <u>Mike Alton's Site Sell</u> blog tips.

Graphics

Okay, I'm a writer, *not* a graphic artist. First to admit I draw stick people. However, I've studied the basics of cover design and color theory because, from a marketing perspective, I need to know what works and what doesn't.

Today I'm talking about having *professional* graphics for your social media headers, as well as on your website and/or blog. Many people simply take a picture, post it, and call it a day. In this world where authors are business owners (and if you don't think you are, that's an issue), you need to be a professional if you want to be treated like one.

Assignment #3:

- How do your headers rate on each channel? Are

they blurry, outdated, not representative of you as a brand? If you feel you need an update, see below:

Each social media channel requires a different size, and the pictures you use must be hi-resolution. Canva has a great guide with many options, or you can hire someone to do it all for you. Jerboa Design Studio does all my graphics (example below), and Emilie Rabitoy does #BookMarketingChat graphics (see @TheRuralVA on Twitter.)

I'm always updating my header because something new is usually happening: a new book coming out, a new project, an award, something. This business is fluid, and you need to be flexible and present.

Keep in mind that your header needs to represent

- Your color story (Mine is red. Duh. :). Purple is my secondary color.)

- Your brand
- Use colors that draw the eye in (Red, purple, blue, are a good start. Gray, tan, and white are dull and flat.)

Visually, you can see that I'm a writer without me *saying* I am. Show don't tell, right?

Fact: People decide in less than one second (in fact, 13 milliseconds) whether to like or follow you *based on your visual.* Make it count.

Unsplash.com has over 600,000 royalty-free images you can use and size as needed until you can customize something unique to you (just remember: everyone else can use them, too).

That's it for today. See you tomorrow.

DAY TWENTY FOUR: SOCIAL MEDIA ICONS, ABOUT PAGE, MEDIA KIT

Yesterday, we discussed Google Analytics and SEO -- I know, it was a lot. I'll keep today kinda short.

Social Media Icons

I don't know about you, but when I go to someone's site or read their blog, if I like their content, I want to share it. Sharing is 1,000 times easier if they have their social media icons and share buttons right there on their post, as well as on their site. (I also have share extensions on my Chrome toolbar, but that's an entirely different topic).

Let me show you what I mean. Below is a screenshot of one of my blog posts.

As you can see, it's very easy for anyone to click on any of the share buttons right above (and below as well, but that's not in the shot) to share my post. Additionally, in the top right, all of my social media follow icons are placed in an easily visible way. They are in that place for a very particular reason: people read left to right, up to down (at least in English-speaking countries).

If your social media icons are like a scavenger hunt, and you are forcing people to go on a search mission to find some way to share your content, forget it. They're gone. You've just lost a reader, and they likely won't be back. This is also affecting your overall website grade and your SEO.

Note: You want to have BOTH *Share* buttons on your blog posts, and *Follow* buttons on your site.

You've *also* lost out on a potentially huge opportunity for reach and engagement -- meaning if they shared your content, all of their followers and readers could see your post and read it, and then their followers and readers could see it and share it, and so on, and so on, and so on.

Assignment #1:

- *Place your social media share **and** follow icons in an easy to find spot on your site,* as well as on each blog post. Make it as easy as possible for your readers to share your work and follow you! (If you're on Wordpress, this is simply a matter of choosing a plug-in that works for your theme.)

About Page

Do you have an *About Page* on your site? Most authors don't. Readers are very curious about writers. Not only what we write, but who we are as people (yet one more reason to build relationships and not blast spammy links).

You don't need to tell them what you eat for dinner (unless

you know, it was super yummy or you're a food writer), but it's a good idea to share:

- some background,
- what types of writing you do (e.g., magazines, nonfiction, short stories, poetry, whatever),
- where else they can find you online,
- show your face -- people want to see your mug
- and, most importantly, where to purchase your books.

True story: an author who shall remain nameless, complained that nobody purchased his book. Oh, did he whine. "My publisher isn't doing anything," and "Nobody reads my work," and "I've done everything possible and yet I've got no sales." So, I visited his site.

Well. The site was a Weebly blog, not SEO optimized in any way, no social media icons whatsoever, and nowhere, anywhere on the site, did he even show his books or link to where readers could purchase them.

Don't be that author.

Assignment #2

- *Create your About Page*, even if it's bare bones. Here, take a look at my <u>Rachel Thompson, Author About Page</u>. Include share buttons as well -- let people share your awesomeness (and feel free to share my About Page if you're so inclined.). Here's a screenshot below as well:

Notice how easy it is for people to share my page, link to my various work, and also purchase my books? Make yours *that* easy, too.

Media Kit

Do you have a media kit? I didn't. I didn't even know I needed to have one until people started asking me for one -- I just kept pulling all of my info together every time someone wanted me to guest blog or I had an interview (and if that hasn't happened for you yet, don't worry -- it will, if you do all the stuff I am advising in this challenge). It was a lot of work I didn't need to do. A media kit organizes all that for you -- saves time.

A media kit can be really complicated or super basic. I keep mine fairly basic, and update it as needed, but you're more than welcome to get fancy. Here's a great guide from the BookMarketingMaven with tips and several examples. You can also create a PDF people can download. Your choice.

To see my media kit, visit Rachel's Media Kit.

That's it for today, challengers.

See you tomorrow.

DAY TWENTY FIVE: OTHER SOCIAL MEDIA SITES AND WHY THEY MATTER: YOUTUBE, PINTEREST, INSTAGRAM

First off, I know y'all were interested in my 30-day Challenge because you're reading this, but have you signed up for my regular **BadRedheadMedia** newsletter? See, I can't automatically add you to that newsletter because of the CAN-SPAM Act (unless I want to be fined $16,000 per person, which hell, no, I do not.), so if you'll kindly take the time to sign up for my regular newsletter, you'll keep up on all my handy tips.

Worth noting: I don't sound out newsletter often. We all get enough darn email. Only for new stuff. Promise.

Here's a link to the form as well as a tweet you can share, please and thank you:

Have you signed up for my @BadRedheadMedia newsletter?
Well, get up on it.
http://ow.ly/YITit #BookMarketingTips #AuthorHelp

Know Thy Demographics

Where are your readers? This question is still confusing to many authors. They just do not know. So, let's discuss demographics today, as well as a few other social channels, and why they could matter to your platform (giving you a break from the website/blog stuff today).

Who exactly is your demographic?

Pew Research

According to the last full survey of social media done by the Pew Research Center in September, 2014 (wow, think how much has already changed since *then*), here's the breakdown by social media channel:

Facebook:

71% of adult internet users/58% of entire adult population

Fully 71% of online American adults use Facebook, a proportion unchanged from August 2013. Usage among seniors continues to increase. Some 56% of internet users ages 65 and older now use Facebook, up from 45% who did so in late 2013 and 35% who did so in late 2012. Women are also particularly likely to use Facebook compared with men, a trend that continues from prior years.

Twitter:

23% of adult internet users/19% of entire adult population

Some 23% of online adults currently use Twitter, a statistically significant increase compared with the 18% who did so in August 2013. Twitter is particularly popular among those under 50 and the college-educated. Compared with late 2013, the service has seen significant increases among a number of demographic groups: men, whites, those ages 65 and older, those who live in households with an annual household income of $50,000 or more, college graduates, and urbanites.

Instagram

26% of adult internet users/21% of entire adult population

Some 26% of online adults use Instagram, up from 17% in late 2013. Almost every demographic group saw a significant increase in the proportion of users. Most notably, 53% of young adults ages 18-29 now use the service, compared with 37% who did so in 2013. Besides young adults, women are particularly likely to be on Instagram, along with Hispanics and African-Americans, and those who live in urban or suburban environments.

Pinterest

28% of adult internet users/22% of entire adult population

Some 28% of online adults use Pinterest, up from the 21% who did so in August 2013. Women continue to dominate the site, as they did in 2013: fully 42% of online women are Pinterest users, compared with just 13% of men (although men did see a significant increase in usership from 8% in 2013). While Pinterest remains popular among younger users, there was an 11-point increase between 2013 and 2014 in the proportion of those 50 and older who use the site. Other demographic groups that saw a notable increase in usership include whites, those living in the lowest- and highest-income households, those with at least some college experience, and suburban and rural residents.

LinkedIn

28% of adult internet users/23% of entire adult population

Some 28% of online adults are LinkedIn users, up from 22% in August 2013. The site continues to be particularly popular among college graduates, those in higher-income households and the employed (although the increase in usage by those who are not employed to 21% from 12% in 2013 is notable). College graduates continue to dominate use of the site. Fully 50% use LinkedIn, a 12-point increase since last year. It is the only platform where those ages 30-64 are more likely to be users than those ages 18-29.

Hopefully, the next update will include sites like Snapchat, Periscope, and other channels which have captured some of the pie. Not sure where YouTube and Google+ are either, as both are owned by Google and clearly critical to our SEO/SMO ranking. Anyway...

Assignment 1:

- Go dig into this report. Somewhere in there is *your*

demographic. Remember, when looking at these Facebook numbers, they are talking about the personal 'friends' accounts, which you cannot 'sell' to. However, you *can* connect to people on a personal level, which is great for building relationships.

Pinterest:

How do I use Pinterest? What is it? Why do I care?

I can't possibly go over all the details here, but here's an excellent basic Pinterest post on Jane Friedman's site -- do everything she says. It's great, and it works.

True story: Pinterest is a huge traffic generator for me. On a recent guest post by ex-rock photographer Michael Strider titled ***This is the Reason Gene Simmons Told Me To Check My Ego,*** I received over 100 pins. For me, that's terrific. (You should read it -- it's a great post and all true.)

Below is a screenshot of my own Pinterest account profile:

Assignment #2:

- *Go create a Pinterest account.* It's easy. If you create *Business* account, you can use Rich Pins (which means you can advertise and add Buy buttons to your pins. See their Help Section for more info on that.). Follow my Rachel Thompson account if you want! Pinterest is *not* about the hard sell. Create boards about topics of interest. It's a visual channel.

StumbleUpon

SU is just one of those weird sites people either love or don't get/really ever use... I didn't for a long time. And then, once I did, *whoa.* I get an enormous amount of traffic to my website from it.

Mostly, I just click on the Stumble button on my Chrome extension, to share posts from all around the net. I also Stumble all of my own posts as soon as I hit publish. I'm careful not to *only* Stumble my own content (they frown on that). Note: This extension can be glitchy and I often have to uninstall and reinstall. Sigh.

You can also go into SU itself to follow others and share content, etc. It's not a traditional social network, in that you don't really talk to people -- it's mostly an aggregator, more about sharing. I probably go into SU itself maybe once every few weeks, though I stumble articles frequently as I go about my day.

Here's a screenshot of my StumbleUpon profile:

Assignment #3:

- *Yep, go create a SU account.* It's very easy. You can follow <u>my StumbleUpon account</u>, too.

That's it for today. See you tomorrow.

DAY TWENTY SIX: BLOGGING --
WHY BOTHER? FREQUENCY,
COSCHEDULE HEADLINE
ANALYZER

I talk a lot about how important blogging is for building our connections with readers. Blogging is also done on our home (website), which we own -- if you only shared blog posts on say, Facebook, I'd caution you, because Facebook can shut down your account at any time (I've seen it done too many times) -- though I do love their new Notes feature and encourage you to share a post or three over there using that functionality.

Let's put a pin in the whole 'building relationships' thing for today and look at some hard facts.

Why is Blogging Important to our Author Platform?

I hear this daily:

- I'm an author, not a blogger
- I don't have time to blog
- Blogging is for amateurs; I'm a professional author
- I don't know what to blog about...writing? Why should I blog about writing when I can *be* writing?

Simple answer: Google loves fresh content.

SEO and Google algorithms are complicated. I'm certainly not an expert, but I do read and research. I've learned that:

- blogging once weekly is sufficient to keep the Google spider crawly things happy;
- longer content is rewarded more than shorter content (no matter how much you argue and stomp your feet about it -- more below)
- social media counts
- you need to tag and link your images (use royalty-free)
- indexed pages -- this is THE most important reason and most of you probably don't know what it means -- I didn't either.

Indexed Pages

*Perhaps the most important reason of all to blog is the fact that each post counts as a new page on your website. Google likes fresh content and will reward those who share frequently. Those who do include a {business} blog on their site will see up to 55% more traffic than companies who don't. The reason for this is the indexed pages. For Google to index those pages, you need to include at least 300 quality words. That means reblogging, short blogs, and duplicating content won't help you much at all. There **is** a time and place for the previously mentioned blog types, but not when you're hoping to boost your SEO. (Source: Business2Community.com, 2014)*

Assignment #1:

- *Read this entire article* (it's short): 9 Reasons Why Blogging Is Essential To Good SEO Results

---

It's worth noting that this information, though valuable, is from 2014. Google's algorithm has changed a few times since then, and they're now rewarding what's called 'long-form' content even more, meaning blog posts that contain 2500-3000 words. This doesn't mean you *must* do that -- do what you want.

I can already hear the whining, and believe me, I've heard it all already:

- *My readers won't read 2000-3000 words!* (Really? How do you know?)
- *When will I have time to work on my book?* (Maybe you trade off. Marketing isn't either/or.)
- *I can't write 2,000 words weekly!* So, don't. Nobody says you have to. Calm down. Write what you can. Just know that Google is giving higher ranking to longer form content.

Assignment #2:

- *Read these two great posts* by Neil Patel and CoSchedule explaining **long-form content** and how you can easily transition to it without exploding that vein popping on your head.

Assignment #3:

- Take a recent headline from one of your blog posts, and copy and paste it over to the CoSchedule Headline Analyzer (I would marry this tool if I could). What's your score? Your goal is 70 or above (e.g., in the green). Because I'm that much of a perfectionist, I shoot for 80 or higher.

Headlines will make or break your post. You can spend thirty minutes writing the best post you've written all year, and then lazily slap on some goofy headline like, "I Hate Paper Apples," (I don't know, maybe you do). How well will that post perform? How many clicks and retweets/shares will you get?

Well, let's just see, shall we?. Let's now take this headline over to the free <u>CoSchedule Headline Analyzer</u>... and we get a score of 41. Wah wah wah. See below:

Work with this awesome free tool until you get a score of 70 or above. Let me try...

...and I'm back. Took me three tries. Ha. "This is the Reason I Hate Paper Apples"

See below:

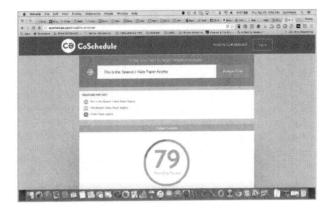

Once you scroll down the page, they give you all kinds of data -- how the headline looks on Google, keywords used, how to shorten or lengthen if needed, unique and common words, and more. The tips alone on writing better headlines are worth using it every time.

I *love love love* this free tool, and I encourage you to use it for every headline you write.

That's it for now.

See you tomorrow.

DAY TWENTY SEVEN: POSTS THAT GO VIRAL, DRIP FEEDS, #MONDAYBLOGS (AGAIN)

How do you make posts go viral?

Wouldn't it be nice to push an easy button to make that happen? Or to know that sweet magic formula? Well, the reality is...readers are fickle. Sometimes a post will spread like wildfire, sometimes it won't. However, there are a few tools of the copywriting trade that any of us can use to help increase our odds of this happening.

True Story: This is my <u>most popular EVER on BadRedheadMedia.com</u>

My most popular post ever: 4 Dumb Ways To Waste Your Writing Time http://ow.ly/YOnuZ via @BadRedheadMedia

and you know why? Anne Rice's assistant saw it on my Face-book page and shared it on *her* Facebook page. Rice herself gave it a ringing endorsement and whoa -- 2500+ shares in one day! *falls over*

Assignment #1: and the most critical point for today:

- Read this awesome post from BoostBlog on how to make your posts go viral. Bookmark it, and every time you write a post, see if your post fits into one of these categories. (I'm not even going to give you any hints because you need to read this post. Go.)

Assignment #2:

What is Triberr?

- Take a look at Triberr. I joined Triberr eons ago and I love it. Most authors don't take the time to figure it out and while it's not difficult, it can take a little bit of reading and training to understand how it works. Basically, you join tribes of like-minded people, connect your Twitter (and other channels if you choose) and blog RSS feed, and share each other's posts automatically (you have settings to decide how often).

Why bother? You can benefit from the reach and engagement of others. It's a brilliant concept and I can't say enough great things about it. It may not be for you. The biggest complaints I've heard are from people who don't take the time to utilize the settings properly, tweeting out others' posts every 15 minutes -- don't do that. I share posts not more than once every three to four hours.

What is <u>Missing Lettr</u>?

- Take a look at this great little site. It's free for one account.

New to the game, Missing Lettr analyzes your latest blog posts and creates a drip feed of tweets with links to the post for you. Just connect your Twitter and blog link and they do the rest. Either approve or don't approve what they send, and they give you the option to edit each tweet and add popular, relevant hashtags.. Takes all of three minutes. I'm liking it so far.

*Note: some people complained about this free service when it first started out. I'm still with them and find it very helpful to share blog posts repeatedly every so often on an automated schedule with different taglines and visuals I've pre-approved. Still worth using or trying again, in my opinion.

Assignment #3:

Participate in #MondayBlogs- Once again, here's the article that explains exactly what it is and why you should be participating:

http://badredheadmedia.com/what-is-mondayblogs-and-why-you-should-be-participating/

Write a non-promotional (non "Read all about my book!") post, share it with the hashtag on Mondays. Pretty easy. Most people see at least 3-4 times their normal traffic, increase Twitter followers, and find that, over time, it's a great reciprocal community. Share your posts, retweet others. Done.

Tip: Schedule in your #MondayBlogs posts at any point during the week using your favorite social media management tool. Why wait until Monday when you're already crazy busy?

The entire point of all these sites and tools is to help increase visibility of your posts, which in turn helps increase your visibility to readers, which in turn raises your SEO and Google ranking and hopefully, and ***all this works together to help sales***.

That's it for today, folks. See you tomorrow.

DAY TWENTY EIGHT: HOW IMPORTANT IS YOUTUBE TO YOUR AUTHOR PLATFORM?

M ost authors, including myself, don't do much with YouTube, but that's a mistake for a lot of reasons, which I'll discuss below.

*****Unless you've been hiding in a cave, or maybe you've forgotten, **Google owns YouTube**. What does this mean for us? Posting videos helps our Google rankings. So yea, we need to be on there. But we need to be on there in an optimized way.*****

Some stats:

- YouTube is the second largest search engine (after Google)
- One Billion unique monthly visitors
- Reaches more U.S. adults ages 18-34 than *any* cable network

(Source: MushroomNetworks.com)

Many of us are introverts -- we like being hidden behind our computers, letting our written words do the talking for us, right? Venturing out in front of the camera is a scary proposition. I get it. While I'm fairly comfortable in front of a group (I was a sales trainer for many years and have done a fair share of public speaking, webinars, and panels), I'll admit, chattering away in front of a camera isn't my first choice.

How important is YouTube for authors, really?

See my hard to miss message above. However, I did a little informal poll on Twitter and Facebook. Keeping it simple, I asked two questions:

How important is YouTube as part of an author's platform -- very important, or not important at all?

Twitter results below:

Facebook results:

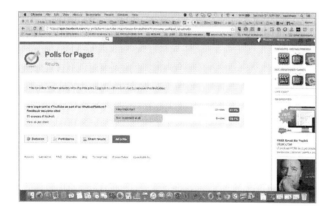

So, totally different answers! Ha.

I'm guessing this is a demographic thing -- Facebook is an older demographic, Twitter younger. Which is kind of confusing, as YouTube skews younger, so I don't know.

The Experts

Assignment #1:

- *Read this:* According to Jeni Chappelle, writing coach and editor, YouTube is very helpful for writers as a visual tool. Use it as an addendum to writing events, interviews, to share your WIP or about to be released book, or even to interview a fan (or have fans interview you). To learn more, check out her fab article on <u>YouTube 101 for Authors</u>.

If you write fiction, here's a really helpful post from <u>BookPromotionHub</u>. It's a bit outdated but the info at the bottom is useful. Even if you write nonfiction as I do, the info is still useful.

Assignment #2:

- Watch this: <u>Marie Forleo (aka Marie TV)</u>

Total pro. More businesswoman than author (though she's that also), you'll learn how to use video to your advantage. She also offers courses in how to create your platform and from what I'm told by author colleagues I know well who have been through her program, while somewhat expensive, worth it.

*Note: not an endorsement.

I like her. She's savvy, funny, and smart. My sister can't stand her. Whatever. Decide for yourself.

Point is, these people are making a living because they use YouTube as part of their platform, which ups their visibility, which ups their -- you guessed it -- Google ranking.

How I'm currently using my <u>YouTube channel</u>: sharing an updated trailer for *Broken Pieces*, working on another book trailer (with a professional guy who does these), and recording teasers for several upcoming books (pre-marketing).

Here's an example tweet (feel free to share) of how I ask others to share my *Broken Pieces* book trailer. Remember, keep it short, not a hard sell, clear about genre, shortened link. *Tip: When asking others to share your tweets, remember to include your own handle.*

Broken   Pieces   by   @rachelintheoc   #video
http://ow.ly/YPLjf ***"I'm not fragile...then again...*I'm not the one who broke"** **#memoir**

That's it for today, friends. See you tomorrow, for our last day together. *sniff*

DAY TWENTY NINE/THIRTY: WRAP-UP

Last day. How to wrap up this entire challenge? I can't, really. We've covered so many different topics, right? I thought I'd go over some of the general questions I've received from some of you from the original newsletter challenge, as well as questions I receive daily online -- some specific, some more general, and hope it helps you, too.

Q: Will using Facebook Notes (on either my personal or page) detract from my blog?
A: No. Some readers are *only* on Facebook. It's like a casino they never leave that entices them with fancy poker chips and free drink coupons. They love it there, it's easy, and they are not going to budge.

However, they might just read one of your Notes and then click over to Amazon to purchase your book. Who knows? Take advantage of the option.

Q: Which is better, Hootsuite or Buffer?
A: I like both, and use both. Hootsuite (the paid version) is my main squeeze, and Buffer is my backup. I don't like Hootsuite's mobile app, while I adore Buffer's. So, I use one on desktop, and one on mobile.

Just space it out, so you're not posting every ten seconds. A few times a day is plenty.

There are many, many social media management tools out there -- I'm simply focused on the two I regularly use. As I mentioned, I try new tools all the time. Explore to find one you prefer and that fits your budget. Bottom line: these handy tools save you time so you have more time to write.

I also highly recommend PromoRepublic because it has everything and I can pre-schedule posts to Instagram. Super convenient.

Q: I did the website grader. Why is my score so low?
A: I don't know. The website grader gives you tools to fix what's wrong, which you can then take to your admin, or if you're your own admin, to figure out what you need to adjust.

Usually, it's something pretty fixable like learning how to SEO-optimize each blog post, placing your social media follow icons on each page *and* sharing icons each post, and such.

If not, check with your host and see what options they suggest.

Do you still feel this way????

Q: How do I get more Twitter followers?
A: We discussed this, and remember, a million Twitter followers means nothing if you're not engaged, or fake, or if they aren't interested in what you're interested in. Listen to your peeps. Ask questions.

I can't tell you how important it is to engage with followers daily, follow using keywords (by purchasing a Pro Plan on ManageFlitter.com ($12/month), you have the option to follow using keywords and key phrases). If you can't afford that, spend the extra time finding *readers*, not following other authors. The biggest mistake authors make is following other authors, and then bitching about all the book spam. That's not Twitter's fault -- that's yours.

To answer this, however: follow people daily, and people will follow you back. Be sure they are readers, book bloggers, book reviewers, and other influencers. *Follow smart.*

Q: How is your book *Broken Pieces* still selling well (eBook version) on Women's Poetry after all this time?
A: I send Amazon Nutella daily. #Kidding.

Is it because of all this marketing I do? Perhaps. It's also a 10-time award winner, has well over 200 reviews (mostly positive), and because I took this opportunity to establish an advocacy platform to help other sexual abuse survivors. I also interact with readers constantly.

The book has legs. I've written a second *Broken* book. I'm now writing a third, *Broken People*. Writing books that resonate with people, connecting with book bloggers and book reviewers, writing well-written books (professionally edited, format-ted, and designed) that garner top reviews, developing the various parts of your platform, helping others, being generous -- *all* of it matters. Most of all, I write what scares me.

Q: What's the difference between Wordpress.org and Word-press.com? Can you explain in one sentence or less?
A: So many differences, and I'm not a web expert. However, here's my one sentence:

Rent (.com) or own (.org = self-hosted), you decide. If you're still confused, reread the section on websites or Google that shit.

Q: What is the deciding factor for a book's success?
A: Let me consult my Magic 8-Ball...

Seriously, who knows? You have to be able to write a good story, have a knowledge of the craft, and respect for yourself and your reader. Trust your voice. Write what scares you. Be grateful.

And accept that nobody owes you anything. It's a privilege when anyone reads our work, let alone shares it or reviews it.

Who are we to criticize a reader, blogger, or reviewer (even if they get it totally wrong)? They spent time on our work.

A little more gratefulness and a little less ego can help any author.

Q: Is blogging really necessary?
A: *Oh my gosh*, are we seriously still having this conversation? Because I refuse to discuss this anymore. Don't blog. Sit in your cave. Wait to be found. Let me know how that goes.

Depends on your goal. If you want readers to find you, if you want Google to index you, if you want your name to show up on search engines for a certain keyword or search term, which can all help your visibility and lead to sales, yes. If you don't think it matters and people will magically find your work because it's so amazing, then I wish you well.

Art is work.

Q: Why do I have to market my books? Why can't I just write?
A: Sigh. Go back to Day One. Do-over.

Q: Why do I need Mailchimp? Can't I just send emails to 100 people at a time?

A: You can, but if one of those reports you for spam (because there's no 'opt-in' with mass emails), it's a $16,000 fine per person. I don't know about you, but I don't have that kind of cash laying around.

Q: Everything you mentioned costs a ton of money. I'm on a limited income. What do you feel are necessities?

A: Silly. No it doesn't. Actually, here's *all the free shit* I mentioned so stop the whining:

- *Twitter,*
- *Facebook page,*
- *G+ Page,*
- *Pinterest*
- *YouTube*
- *Instagram*
- *and a blog are all free.*
- *Mailchimp*
- *AuthorMarketingClub.com is a free site to list your free books*
- *BookBub author listing is also free.*
- *Freebooksy's author widget for FB is free.*
- *Woobox for FB tags -- free.*
- *Hootsuite free option*
- *Buffer free option*
- *Pablo by Buffer (to create visuals), free.*
- *ManageFlitter free option*

- *Triberr, free.*
- *Missing Lettr, free.*

I'm tired. There's more. Go back through this book for more free stuff.

What costs:

- A hosted website with a domain you own is about $12 for the domain for the year,
- and $8/month for the hosting.
- A theme can run from free to $60 or more.
- Hootsuite Pro: $9.99/month.
- ManageFlitter Pro: $12/month
- BookMarketingTool.com: $29.00 to list a free book
- Many paid newsletter sites (listed throughout the challenge), like FreeBooksy, BargainBooksy, Kindle Nation Daily, BookBub, etc., are not free but affordable, depending on your budget and sales goals.

It's really up to you how, when, or if to spend your marketing dollars. That's what this all comes down to. Remember, this as well: being an author is a business. *These are business expenses.* Consult a CPA on how much you can deduct from your income.

Fear and laziness are the biggest roadblocks to success -- people say it's time, but I disagree. I'm just as busy as you, we're all just as busy as each other, yet somehow some of us are doin' the damn thing. Want it? Do the work.

CONCLUSION

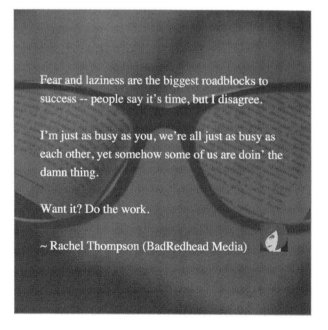

Fear and laziness are the biggest roadblocks to success -- people say it's time, but I disagree.

I'm just as busy as you, we're all just as busy as each other, yet somehow some of us are doin' the damn thing.

Want it? Do the work.

~ Rachel Thompson (BadRedhead Media)

If you haven't yet, please subscribe to my regular <u>BadRedhead Media newsletter</u> to keep up on all my book marketing tips and news.

And if you haven't yet followed me on social media, here's where to find me:

Twitter: http://twitter.com/BadRedheadMedia
Facebook: <u>https://www.facebook.com/BadRedheadMedia/</u>
Pinterest: https://www.pinterest.com/badredheadmedia/
Google+:
https://plus.google.com/u/0/109753040545970395194/posts

and I appreciate any shout-outs, love, retweets, shares, or spare Nutella. Thanks, everyone!

Thank you for spending your time with me. I appreciate your purchase and would love it if you'd take a few minutes to *review this book* on Amazon (and Goodreads). As you know, readers decide to purchase a book based on word of mouth, and your opinion counts.

Stay tuned for my next challenges, author friends. *The BadRedhead Media 30-Day Twitter Challenge* is next.

Contact me anytime and see below for a thorough list of help and resources mentioned throughout the book.

Rachel Thompson:

Amazon Author Central - http://www.amazon.com/Rachel-Thompson/e/B004KTY7Q0
BadRedhead Media Newsletter - http://eepurl.com/koN8r
BadRedheadMedia.com - http://badredheadmedia.com/
Broken Pieces Book Trailer https://www.youtube.com/watch?v=3BK2_hterRU
Facebook - https://www.facebook.com/BadRedheadMedia/
Facebook - https://www.facebook.com/BookMarketingChat
Facebook - https://www.facebook.com/RachelThompsonauthor/
Facebook Notes -https://www.facebook.com/notes/rachel-thompson/weve-lived-in-shame-long-enough/1068072763226665 Google+
https://plus.google.com/u/0/109753040545970395194/posts
Medium - https://medium.com/@RachelintheOC
Pinterest - https://www.pinterest.com/rachelintheoc/
Rachel Thompson About - http://rachelintheoc.com/about/
Rachel Thompson Media Kit - http://rachelintheoc.com/media-kit/
RachelintheOC.com - http://rachelintheoc.com/
StumbleUpon - http://www.stumbleupon.com/stumbler/RachelintheOC
Twitter - https://twitter.com/badredheadmedia
Twitter - https://twitter.com/BkMarketingChat
Twitter - http://twitter.com/mondayblogs
Twitter - http://twitter.com/RachelintheOC

YouTube -
https://www.youtube.com/channel/UCZQevHGrKTwrjqlPLpO
xcig

Other Contacts:

Barb Drozdowich/Bakerview Consulting-
http://bakerviewconsulting.com/
Barb Drozdowich/*The Author's Guide to Working with Book
Bloggers* My Book
Barb Drozdowich/ Book Blogger List
http://bookbloggerlist.com/
Jah Kaine/ Jerboa Design Studio http://jerboadesignstudio.com/
Emilie Rabitoy Twitter- http://twitter.com/TheRuralVA

RESOURCES

Twitter https://twitter.com/
Twitter Support https://twitter.com/Support @Support
Twitter Support https://support.twitter.com/
Twitter Support /Signing up with Twitter
https://support.twitter.com/articles/100990
Twitter Support/ Advanced Search
https://support.twitter.com/articles/71577
Twitter Support/ Using Twitter Lists
https://support.twitter.com/articles/76460
Twitter Support/ Request to Verify an Account
https://support.twitter.com/articles/20174631
Twitter Blog https://blog.twitter.com/
TweetChat http://tweetchat.com/
Twubs http://twubs.com/
Bit.ly https://bitly.com/
Bit.ly About https://bitly.com/pages/about
ManageFlitter https://manageflitter.com/
ManageFlitter Plans https://manageflitter.com/pro

Hootsuite https://hootsuite.com/

Hootsuite Plans https://hootsuite.com/plans/free

Google Support/Create an Alert
https://support.google.com/alerts/answer/4815696?hl=en

GooglePlus Support/ About
https://support.google.com/plus/answer/1710600?hl=en

Google Analytics https://www.google.com/analytics/

Google+ Pages/About
https://support.google.com/plus/answer/1710600?hl=en

Google/ Pop-Up Rules
http://mashable.com/2016/08/23/google-pop-up-mobile-search-results/#.m7Z4UKbYSq5

Flipboard https://flipboard.com/

Scoop.it http://www.scoop.it/

BrainPickings https://www.brainpickings.org/

Buffer Blog https://blog.bufferapp.com/

CoSchedule http://coschedule.com/

CoSchedule/ Headline Analyzer
http://coschedule.com/headline-analyzer

Klout https://klout.com/home

Woobox https://woobox.com/

Pinterest https://www.pinterest.com/

Pew Research Center http://www.pewresearch.org/

Hubspot http://blog.hubspot.com/marketing?
_ga=1.197072618.739249614.1454606891

Alexa http://www.alexa.com/

Alexa/ Chrome Extension
https://chrome.google.com/webstore/detail/alexa-traffic-rank/cknebhggccemgcnbidipinkifmmegdel?hl=en

FreeBooksy Author Marketing App
https://www.freebooksy.com/freebooksy-author-marketing-ap/

FreeBooksy https://www.freebooksy.com/freebooksy-feature-pricing/

BargainBooksy
https://www.bargainbooksy.com/sell-more-books/

BookBuzzer http://www.bookbuzzr.com/plans.php

WiseStamp http://www.wisestamp.com/

Facebook Terms of Service
https://www.facebook.com/legal/terms?pnref=story

Facebook Create a Page https://www.facebook.com/pages/create/

Facebook Create a Page Username
https://www.facebook.com/username

Facebook Help/ Verification Form
https://www.facebook.com/help/contact/356341591197702

AllIndieWriters/ Marketing Plan Outline
http://allindiewriters.com/free-book-marketing-plan-outline/

AllIndieWriters/ Book Marketing Timeline
http://allindiewriters.com/book-marketing-timeline-from-pre-launch-to-post-launch/

Joanna Penn/Free Marketing Plan
http://www.thecreativepenn.com/wp-content/uploads/2009/02/marketing_plan.pdf

BookMarketingTools.com http://bookmarketingtools.com/

Medium - https://medium.com/

UnSplash https://unsplash.com/

BookMarketingMaven/ How to Create a Media Kit
http://bookmarketingmaven.typepad.com/ezine/book-marketing-march-2010.html

Pablo by Buffer https://pablo.buffer.com/

Amazon Author Central/ About
https://authorcentral.amazon.com/gp/help?topicID=200497410

Amazon/ Giveaway

https://www.amazon.com/gp/giveaway/home/ref=author_tools
_giveaway_acnov15

Amazon/ Giveway FAQ https://www.amazon.com/b/?
_encoding=UTF8&node=11715260011

Amazon/ KDP Select https://kdp.amazon.com/help?
topicId=A6KILDRNSCOBA

Amazon/ Kindle Countdowns https://kdp.amazon.com/help?
topicId=A3288N75MH14B8

Amazon/ Kindle Unlimited https://kdp.amazon.com/help?
topicId=AA9BSAGNO1YJH

Amazon/ Giveaway Intro Video
https://www.youtube.com/watch?
v=B5NWkdzNZM0&feature=youtu.be

Amazon/ Advertising for KDP Select
https://kdp.amazon.com/help?topicId=A2DJUTY13KIH2C

CAN SPAM ACT https://www.ftc.gov/tips-advice/business-
center/guidance/can-spam-act-compliance-guide-business

Book Reviews/Publisher's Weekly
http://www.publishersweekly.com/pw/by-topic/authors/pw-
select/article/64936-book-review-success-for-indie-
authors.html

Book Reviews/Your Writer Platform
http://www.yourwriterplatform.com/get-reviews-
for-your-book/

Book Reviews/Book Blogger List http://bookbloggerlist.com/

Book Reviews/ YA Book Blog Directory
http://yabookblogdirectory.blogspot.ca/

Book Reviews/Story Cartel http://storycartel.com/?
utm_content=bufferba61b&utm_medium=social&utm_source=
facebook.com&utm_campaign=buffer

Book Reviews/ Mandy Boles

http://www.mandyboles.com/2012/01/directory-of-book-bloggers-on-pinterest/

Book Reviews/ Kate Tilton http://katetilton.com/kate-tiltons-book-bloggers/

Book Reviews/ Indie Reviewers http://www.theindieview.com/indie-reviewers/

Book Reviews/ Step by Step Publishing http://www.stepbystepselfpublishing.net/reviewer-list.html

TheBalance/ 6 Steps for Publishing Success https://www.thebalance.com/advance-book-marketing-2799978

MailChimp http://mailchimp.com/

MailChimp/ Facebook Intergration http://kb.mailchimp.com/integrations/facebook/add-or-remove-a-signup-form-on-your-facebook-page

Website.Grader.com https://website.grader.com/

Lori Culwell/ How to Make a Website in 6 Minutes or Less https://www.youtube.com/watch?v=pxpGntD_3KA

Lori Culwell & Katherine Sears /How to Market a Book My Book

PC World/ How to Register Your Own Domain http://www.pcworld.com/article/241722/how_to_register_your_own_domain_name.html

WP Beginner/ How to Switch from Blogger to WordPress http://www.wpbeginner.com/wp-tutorials/how-to-switch-from-blogger-to-wordpress-without-losing-google-rankings/

Canva - https://www.canva.com/create/social-media-graphics/

ClickZ/ Guide - Useful Metrics to Measure Content Marketing Success https://www.clickz.com/25-useful-metrics-to-measure-content-marketing-success/93436/

PewInternet.org Social Media Update 2014 http://www.pewinternet.org/2015/01/09/social-media-update-2014/

Tribber http://triberr.com/
MissingLettr https://missinglettr.com/
Marie Forleo https://www.youtube.com/user/marieforleo
Jenni Chappelle
http://www.jenichappelle.com/2014/06/youtube-writers-101/
Mushroom Networks/ Infographics
https://www.mushroomnetworks.com/infographics/youtube---
the-2nd-largest-search-engine-infographic
Smart Blogger Cheat Sheet for Writing Blog Posts That Go
Viral https://smartblogger.com/go-viral/?
inf_contact_key=8d7550a8a01340992d5dffb0042f66b31b5918
9f92b46e3d1a7b60ee9350f05e

BadRedhead Media articles referenced:

Thompson, R. (2013. Dec. 31) What Is #MondayBlogs and
Why Should Bloggers Participate?
http://badredheadmedia.com/2013/12/31/mondayblogs-
participate/

Thompson, R. What is #MondayBlogs and Why You Should
Be Participating http://badredheadmedia.com/what-is-
mondayblogs-and-why-you-should-be-participating/

Flickinger, M. (2016. Sept. 2) Twitter Chats for Writers: How
to Get Started by @MelissaFlicks.
http://badredheadmedia.com/2016/09/02/twitter-chats-for-
writers/

BadRedheadMedia.com/ Twitter Posts:
http://badredheadmedia.com/?s=Twitter+

Thompson, R. (2016. Jul. 13). This Is The Reason Your
#Author Platform Impacts Book Sales
http://ow.ly/iKzv302jVHP

Giacolone, J. (2013. Jul. 18). A Champagne Business Plan on a
Beer Wallet. http://badredheadmedia.com/2013/07/18/a-
champagne-business-plan-on-a-beer-wallet-by-guest-
joegiacalone/

Flickinger, M. (2016. Jul. 22). Difference Between Beta-
Readers and ARC Readers: What You Need To Know.
http://badredheadmedia.com/2016/07/22/difference-between-
betareaders-and-arc-readers-what-you-need-to-know-by-
melissaflicks/

Thompson, R. (2016. Mar. 5) This is How You Find Your
Readers. http://badredheadmedia.com/2016/03/05/this-is-how-
you-find-your-readers/

Thompson, R. (2014. Aug. 17). How Do You Build An Audience Before You Have A Product? A Guide.
http://badredheadmedia.com/2014/08/17/how-do-you-build-an-
audience-before-you-have-a-product/

Thompson, R. (2015. Nov. 14) Book Marketing Tips You Need
to Know Now, Part Two!.
http://badredheadmedia.com/2015/11/14/book-marketing-tips-
you-need-to-know-now-part-two/

Drozdowich, B. (2015. Jun. 28). Why WordPress is the Best Choice for your Author Website. http://badredheadmedia.com/2015/06/28/why-wordpress-is-the-best-choice-for-your-author-website/

Thompson, R. (2014. Jan.28) 4 Dumb Ways To Waste Your Writing Time. http://badredheadmedia.com/2014/01/28/stop-wasting-time-write-already/

Articles/Blog Posts:

Fishkin, R. (2015, Dec. 18). The Beginner's Guide to SEO. Moz.com https://moz.com/beginners-guide-to-seo

Long, M.C. (2013, May. 17). How TrueTwit Helps You Help It Make Money – And Waste A Ton Of Time. AdWeek.com. http://www.adweek.com/socialtimes/truetwit/483046

Oliver, A. (2016, Jan. 9). Creating Calls to Action for Social Media That Actually Convert. Canva.com. https://designschool.canva.com/blog/call-to-action/

Lopez, N. (2015). Twitter now lets you pin tweets to the top of your profile on iOS and Android. TheNextWeb.com. http://thenextweb.com/twitter/2015/08/27/twitter-now-lets-you-pin-tweets-to-the-top-of-your-profile-on-ios-and-android/#gref

Wilson, M. (2015. Oct. 28) Now you can follow up to 5,000 people on Twitter -- if you're insane. BetaNews.com.

http://betanews.com/2015/10/28/now-you-can-follow-up-to-5000-people-on-twitter-if-youre-insane

Linchpinseo.com. Twitter Cheat Sheet To Increase Engagement And Followers. Infographic. http://linchpinseo.com/infographic-twitter-tweet-cheat-sheet

Kirkpatrick, M. (2011. Feb. 4) The First Hashtag Ever Tweeted on Twitter – They Sure Have Come a Long Way. Read-Write.com http://readwrite.com/2011/02/04/the_first_hashtag_ever_tweeted_on_twitter_-_they_s/

Sprung, R. (2013. Feb. 21) How to Use Hashtags in Your Social Media Marketing. SocialMediaExaminer.com. http://www.socialmediaexaminer.com/hashtags/

Lee, K. (2015. Oct. 15) 500,000 Beautiful Social Media Images Later: Introducing Pablo 2.0, Perfect Images to Fit All Networks. Blog.Bufferapp.com. https://blog.bufferapp.com/pablo-images-for-instagram-pinterest-twitter-facebook

Allton, M. (2016). Finalists: Top 10 Social Media Blogs 2016 by Social Media Examiner. List.ly. http://list.ly/list/zoo-finalists-top-10-social-media-blogs-2016-by-social-media-examiner?utm_campaign=listlytoday&utm_medium=email&utm_source=listly

Allton, M. (2015. Oct. 27). 19 Search Engine Optimization Tips for Solopreneurs. SiteSell.com.

http://www.sitesell.com/blog/2015/10/19-search-engine-optimization-tips-for-solopreneurs.html

Hines, K. (2012. Aug. 8). An In-Depth Look at the Science of Twitter Timing. KissMetrics.com. https://blog.kissmetrics.com/the-science-of-twitter-timing/

Kolowich, L. (2016. Jan. 11). 20 Fascinating Things You Didn't Know About Your Facebook News Feed. HubSpot.com. http://blog.hubspot.com/marketing/facebook-news-feed-features-facts

Curtis, K. (2015. Nov. 12). Should Google+ Marketing (Still) Be a Part of Your Digital Strategy?. Contentfac.com. http://www.contentfac.com/is-google-marketing-still-important/

Shirvington, M. (2014. Jul. 14). 11 Ways to Get More Followers for Your Google+ Business Page. SocialMediaExaminer.com. http://www.socialmediaexaminer.com/google-plus-business-page-follower-count/

Penn, J. (2012. Oct. 12). Help! My Book Isn't Selling. 10 Questions You Need To Answer Honestly If You Want To Sell More Books. TheCreativePenn.com. http://www.thecreativepenn.com/2012/10/12/help-my-book-isnt-selling/

King, S. (2015. May. 11) A Guest Blog from Stephen King—Yes, that Stephen King. JerryJenkins.com. http://www.jerryjenkins.com/guest-blog-from-stephen-king/

MacLeod, C. K. (2014. Mar. 19). 5 Things You Should Know about Working with Beta Readers. TheBookDesigner.com. http://www.thebookdesigner.com/2014/03/5-things-you-should-know-about-working-with-beta-readers/

Renner, J. (2015. Jun. 6). Questions for Your Beta Readers – and To Focus Your Own Revisions. JaniceHardy.com. http://blog.janicehardy.com/2015/06/questions-for-your-beta-readers-and-to.html

Hines, K. (2016. Feb. 10.) Medium for Business: The Complete Guide for Marketers. SocialMediaExaminer.com. http://www.socialmediaexaminer.com/medium-for-business-the-complete-guide-for-marketers/

(2016. Jan.) Amazon Link Anatomy - For Authors And Publishers.K-lytics.com. Video. http://k-lytics.com/video-vault/amazon-link-anatomy-for-books/

Kiste, G. (2016, Feb. 12.) How Writers Ruin Their Amazon Links (Yes, You Probably Do It Too).gwendolynkiste.com. http://www.gwendolynkiste.com/Blog/how-writers-ruin-their-amazon-links-yes-you-probably-do-it-too/

Jewel, C. (2016. Jan. 31). Amazon Reviews and Timestamps. CarolynJewel.com. http://carolynjewel.com/wordpress/2016/01/31/amazon-reviews-and-timestamps/

Godin, S. (2006. Aug. 6) Advice for Authors. SethGodin.Type-pad.com.

http://sethgodin.typepad.com/seths_blog/2006/08/advice_for_a
uth.html

Nightengale, R. (2014. Apr. 28) 8 Things Most People Don't
Know about Amazon's Best Seller Rank
http://www.makeuseof.com/tag/8-things-people-dont-know-
amazons-bestsellers-rank-sales-rank/

Doctorow, C. (2010. Mar. 4). Free ebooks correlated with
increased print-book sales.
http://boingboing.net/2010/03/04/free-ebooks-correlat.html

Medium.com (2015. Jul. 14). Why Give Your Work Away for
Free?. https://medium.com/medium-writing-prompts/why-
give-away-your-work-for-free-5ed4513d5fa8#.esqy9qbz3

Gonzalo. (2016. Jan. 14). Why People Love Great Visuals,
Based on Science. Pictochart.com.
http://piktochart.com/blog/why-people-love-great-visuals-
science/

Oliphant, K. (2016. Feb. 22) Pinterest for Authors: A Beginner's Guide. JaneFriedman.com.
https://janefriedman.com/how-authors-can-use-pinterest/

Strider, M. (2016, Feb. 7). This is the Reason Gene Simmons
Told Me To Check My Ego. RachelintheOC.com.
http://rachelintheoc.com/2016/02/this-is-the-reason-gene-
simmons-told-me-to-check-my-ego/

Moon, G. (2014. Feb. 12) 5 Things That Will Change Your

Mind About Long Form Content Marketing. CoSchedule.com.
http://coschedule.com/blog/long-form-content/

Patel, N. (2015. Nov. 26) Why You Need to Create Evergreen
Long Form Content and How to Produce It. ttp://neilpatel.-
com/2015/11/26/why-you-need-to-create-evergreen-long-form-
content-and-how-to-produce-it/

Barry, J. (2014. May. 2) 9 Reasons Why Blogging Is Essential
To Good SEO Results. Business2community.com.
http://www.business2community.com/seo/9-reasons-blogging-
essential-good-seo-results-0866944#qtMToXp7MPzeqwpI.99

ACKNOWLEDGMENTS

The idea for this challenge started as a tiny kernel one day as I spoke with several writers in one of my Facebook groups. They expressed frustration at the sheer amount of book marketing they need to do, and were a total loss where to start.

I completely understood.. When I published my first book in early 2011, I wish I'd had a primer of how to do all this *stuff.* Is it helpful? Does it really matter? What's an SEO?

Yes, yes, and we'll get to that.

Drawing on my own years of experiences in publishing, marketing and sales, I put this 30-day challenge together with these three goals:

· It wouldn't be so overwhelming,
· It would be in doable, bite-size pieces,
· It would be practical.

I put together the challenge based on my years as an author, book marketing consultant and social media trainer, and figured I'd offer it completely free for the month of February 2016 (yea, I know, it was a short month but believe me, they got their thirty days worth), to whomever signed up via a special 'challenge' newsletter I created specifically for this purpose.

To my surprise, over 1200 people signed up.

This book would not exist without their feedback, months (and months) of rewrites, multiple updates from all of the various channels (thanks, social media), checks and re-checks of all the various links, and most importantly, the incredibly helpful feedback from over fifty beta-readers, and the diligent attention and amazing skill of my former author assistant and copy editor, Melissa Flickinger.

So, a sincere thank you to all my original challenge takers, dedicated readers, writers, bloggers, reviewers, beta-readers, *and* my dedicated street team who totally rock.

My team, who help me to not lose my mind: Barb Drozdowich, Bobbi Parish, Emilie Rabitoy, C Streetlights, and Jah Kaine;

my whipsmart kids, Anya and Lukas, for the generous hugs too numerous to count, and understanding why Mom doesn't cook very often, and I can't forget my #BookMarketingCats Squeaker and Pip, for their wonderful, calming snuggles.

To all the aspiring authors out there, I've been where you are. I've felt that bewilderment. This book is for you.

ABOUT THE AUTHOR

Rachel Thompson is the author of the award-winning, best-selling *Broken Places* (one of IndieReader's "Best of 2015" top books and 2015 Honorable Mention Winner in both the Los Angeles and the San Francisco Book Festivals), and the best-selling, multi award-winning *Broken Pieces (*as well as two additional humor books. Rachel's work is also featured in several anthologies (see *Books* for details). Rachel released the *BadRedhead Media 30-Day Book Marketing Challenge* in December 2016 to rave reviews.

She owns BadRedhead Media, creating effective social media and book marketing campaigns for authors. Her articles appear regularly in *The Huffington Post, Feminine Collective, Indie Reader The Verbs for Pronoun Publishing, Medium, OnMogul, Transformation Is Real, Blue Ink Review, Book Machine*, and several others.

Not just an advocate for sexual abuse survivors, Rachel is the creator and founder of the hashtag phenomenon #Monday-Blogs and the live weekly Twitter chats, #SexAbuseChat, co-hosted with certified therapist/survivor, Bobbi Parish (Tuesdays, 6pm PST/9pm EST), and #BookMarketingChat, co-hosted with author assistant Emilie Rabitoy (Wednesdays, 6pm PST/9pm EST). Twitter- http://twitter.com/TheRuralVA

She hates walks in the rain, running out of coffee, and coconut. A single mom, she lives in California with her two kids and two cats, where she daydreams of Thor and vaguely remembers what sleep is.

For contact information, visit rachelintheoc.com or **BadRedhead Media** at badredheadmedia.com.

ALSO BY RACHEL THOMPSON

Broken Pieces (Essays Inspired By Life)

5/5 Stars Readers' Favorite Review Winner

2013 eFestival of Words Best Non-Fiction (General) Winner

2014 Kindle Book Award Non-Fiction Finalist

2013 eBook Cover Design Award Gold Star Winner

2013 San Francisco Book Festival Honorable Mention

2013 Global eBook Award Women Studies Non-Fiction Gold Medal Winner

Not easy subjects -- childhood sexual abuse, love, loss, date rape, grief -- but real ones, told in pieces (thus the title). Broken Pieces is a work of non-fiction.

Poetry, prose, and essays to let you into one woman's life -- a searingly raw examination of topics most people avoid.

Already an international #1 best seller on Amazon (eBooks) on Women's Poetry and Abuse, this book is recommended for mature audiences only due to adult themes. For more of Rachel's work, look at Rachel's second award-winning book, Broken Places, which continues the story.

Broken Places A Memoir of Abuse by Rachel Thompson

2016 Bronze Winner Readers' Favorite (NonFiction)

5/5 Stars Readers' Favorite Review Winner

2015 Best of Books, IndieReader (NonFiction)

2015 Honorable Mention Winner Los Angeles Book Festival

2015 Honorable Mention Winner San Francisco Book Festival

Award-winning author Rachel Thompson courageously confronts the topics of sexual abuse and suicide, love and healing, in her second nonfiction book of prose: Broken Places. The sequel to Rachel's first award-winning, best-selling nonfiction book, Broken Pieces, Rachel bares her soul in essays, poems and prose, addressing life's most difficult topics with honesty. As you follow one woman's journey through the dark and into the light, you will find yourself forever changed.

Rachel's first book in this series, Broken Pieces, has been a #1 best seller on Amazon (eBooks) on Women's Poetry and Abuse. Please note: this book discusses serious topics, and is intended for mature audiences only.

One of IndieReader's "Best of 2015" top books and 2015 Honorable Mention Winner in both the Los Angeles and the San Francisco

Book Festivals, in addition to several other awards, Broken Places will capture your mind, body, and soul.

Buffer blog

Made in the USA
Lexington, KY
21 November 2018